SNAKES ON A TRAIN

IN CANADA

MATTHEW ABRA
RYAN SMITH

Snakes on a Train in Canada

ISBN 978-1-4357-3201-8
Copyright © 2008 Standard Copyright License

Language: English
Country: Canada

Dedicated to the six week boys of 2008

...five dollars per dedication please!

Snakes on a Train in Canada

Forward:

Oh! Hello. Didn't see you there, reading our book. Come on in...to the book. Have a triscuit.

Before you dig into the main course, please allow this brief digression into the follies of verve; the vigor and vitality of capitalist enterprise; plainly, please leave room for this utterance towards the shallow graves that we as a society now find ourselves dormant within. For we, as the two individuals responsible for this book, are Transylvanian vampires; bloodsuckers who sleep by day and prey by night, sinking our teeth - our razor sharp, long, and venomous teeth - into the flesh of vanity. We are the *snakes*.

Our prey on this day is superficiality. Our goal is peace on earth and good will towards men (women too, I guess). Our focus, for now, will be on chivalry.

Chivalry is an interesting thing. There are those who might call chivalry mutually exclusive with feminism, but alas, these unfortunate souls have yet to see the bigger picture, and fail to properly deviate to history's progressive past. Chivalry has existed for centuries, while feminism, in all its glory as a leaper of tall buildings, is fundamentally new; an extension of the ideological refuge found in the purity of knighthood, the purity of chivalry.

You may be hard pressed to believe that these basic understandings came to us only recently, while we indulged in the arduous, yet equally virtuous universe of a harlequin romance novel. This very novel, to remain unnamed, looked back on middle age romance as ground zero for all forms of initiative. It began, of course, with the most traditional of the initiations – the knighting. As the sword gently met the shoulders of our heroic male centerpiece, launching his career of servitude for all things honourable and unadulterated, it was only natural that his mind would wander to another sword, the one located in his pants, or "trousers" as they were elegantly referenced. The first few seconds of his knighthood were swimming with so much testosterone and exhilaration, the frenzy was shared by more than his mind. Ultimately, our knight would stand from his kneeling position and reveal to all this unholy animation, an erection so vast, so unequivocal, that it would later earn the name *The New Tower of London.*

It would seem that the knighting of a nobleman acted as the middle age equivalent to Viagra. Our knight would go on to maintain his playful wooden sword for the better part of a week. He treated it as a symbol of excellence, a triumphant roar of showmanship. At the time, it would stand as the only weapon he needed in battle.

But as day six of the supreme joviality came upon our knight, and with no end in sight, it became somewhat apparent to him that this hardening of his nobility was meant for a greater purpose. He was to use it for yet another knighting. So what did the knight do? He went and found a virgin, of course.

That very night, he found a stack of hay near an old country house and lay his subject down in its soft, yet undeniably smelly embrace. The smell was certainly a surprise. No erotic tale had ever prepared him for that one. But ultimately, he persevered, and with the fruit of his loins, he used his prickly new weapon and destroyed the boundaries of her chastity with one all engrossing thrust.

And that was all it took.

As he withdrew, his manhood lowered, and he was void of his weapon once again. The woman had had her initiation. The very sword that had garnered our knight his purity had taken the purity away from another. And from it all, a simple message – a woman's sexual promiscuity seems to rightfully parallel a man's need for honour and superiority. In essence, her "first time" is also her knighting. Yet while the male is given the right to bear arms, the woman is only given the right to bear children. What a world they lived in.

What a deeply superficial world.

Jumping ahead almost a thousand years to the present day, suddenly feminism has taken chivalry's place. Suddenly that very callous condemnation of women and they're need for a sharp christening sword has been replaced by a new ounce of progression. So yes, the harlequin romance is in fact dated, sexist, and even superficial. But it stands to wonder if that superficiality was sparked by the age in which the stories are based, a time when sex was as much a right of passage as it was an excuse for truly cheesy exercises in masculinity.

So, the times have changed, but oh how they have also stayed the same. Indeed, we are no less superficial today than we were a century ago; we are no more invested in the deep causal assaults on society than a knight who flatters his time with premature evacuation. We are stuck in an abyss, but undeniably, a very shallow one.

Therefore, it is without surprise that not too long ago, we, the authors of this story, found ourselves face to face with the beast that is shallow business practice. In this instance, the beast took the form of a snake. A very large snake. A snake that actually had the girth to devour an entire train, as if it were deep-throating a sword inaccessible to William Wallace himself.

On one of our many trips to the movie store, we perused the shelves with or usual fashion of apathy and indignation. It is unusual to find a film unseen by us that holds all the mandatory necessities for a night well wasted. In holding true to the superficial world we exist as a part of, we decided that the Academy Awards section was too deep, the running times in the drama section too long, and naturally, everything in the foreign section too subtitled.

Ultimately our attention would turn to the action section, and after carefully judging every movie by its cover, we settled on as trivial and small-minded a title as we could find – *Snakes on a Train.* Not to be confused with its mile high counterpart, *Snakes on a Plane,* this was to be the simple story of a bunch of people getting bitten by snakes on a locomotive traveling from Mexico to Los Angeles. Or, at least that is what the description on the back suggested.

When the two of us arrived home and popped the gleaming silver disc into our player, we were treated to something much more bizarre; much more incomprehensible. And by "treated" I actually mean crucified. Or maybe even "crucified" is the wrong word. If Jesus died for our sins, then watching this movie was more like dying whilst sinning.

We turned it off after twenty minutes. We could go no further once we had witnessed "the bald man", as we have come to know him, emptily hitting on a "hot chick." His choice for flattery was laughter. He just kept laughing. He would not stop. And then, the "hot chick" joined in. She began laughing with him in a wisp of flirtation. It was a truly dubious pick-up scene. It parted with the realm of realism right from the get go, not because the actors were terrible (and by all accounts, they were), but because the scene failed to concede the very real superficial truths we all know and live by – a "hot chick" does not laugh with a "bald man." How dare a film, one that treated superficiality like an event equal to Christmas, try to mess with this very basic formula. Was it trying to express some hints that it wasn't shallow? Was it attempting to plant the seeds of a message that we are wrong in this manner of thinking? No, more likely "the bald man" was a friend of the producer; a producer who more than likely walked away with a fair bit of money after the fact.

The truth is, pick-up scenes are not conducive to trains. Lest we forget the truly bizarre scene that took place between Frank Sinatra and Janet Leigh in *The Manchurian Candidate*. In it, Sinatra used laze and sweat as his weapons of sweet-talk. Visions of this scene played in my head as I watched "the bald man." Truly, he was doomed from the get go. Not doomed to fail. We do not know if he ever did manage to attain the girl. We did not finish the movie. No, he was doomed in our minds. In a way, it almost felt like we were never meant to get past that scene. If there was indeed a message, it read like this – you are idiots, we took your money, and now you're watching this shit we have created. We were *The Man Churning Candidate*'s, the two chosen for this experiment in capitalist rhythm and force. Truly, the "fat man" made our two manly stomach's churn. He was doomed as the source of our nightmares; the very thing which we have grown to hate. Now "the fat man" will live the rest of his life as our innovative muse. For what you are about to read is inspired by him, and the countless others who took time out of their lives to create *Snakes on a Train*, a monstrosity of immensity only matched by the profit they probably took away from it.

The pick-up scene ended, and so did our evening. We pressed stop. We sat back and breathed. We were still alive. Somehow the guillotine had rusted before encroaching on the nape of our necks. As the two of us turned to one another and looked at the terror in our eyes, a single and communal thought invaded us. "We could write that better."

And so we did.

The very next day we began our version. We wrote briskly, we wrote urgently, but we also wrote very poorly. If there is to be a third author credited for this work, it would be a fine Chardonnay. Wine was our best friend over the course of our writing, which will be quite clearly evident before you have completed the first chapter. But do not be fooled, we also wrote with passion. Our driving force was our ideals; our left-wing pursuit of less bloodshed in this world. Greed and power may be the catalyst for the invasion of countries, but never forget the invasion of the mind. Our psyche had been viciously attacked, and we were on a mission of revenge.

Be warned, the story that follows in not about chivalry and it is not about feminism. It is not about sluts, or the male equivalent, which is still mysteriously missing a name. It is not about business, capitalism, or lesbianism. And it absolutely, most certainly, is not about sex.

But also be assured, all of these things are featured very prominently.

What we have created is, in actuality, a product. It is something for which you can walk into a store - be it movie or book - carrying wads of cash, pick off the shelf - harlequin or action - lay before a young cashier, and pay for. But also be assured, you will never see that money again. It will go to us. It will go to us and everyone else who had a hand in its production.

And one final assurance – you will in fact want that money back. For what you are about to read is not good. It is terrible. It is, quite possibly, the most outlandish, the most preposterous, and the most horribly written thing you could possibly imagine. You will feel dumber after reading it. You may even feel sick. We lobbied with our publisher to provide a free barf bag with every purchase, but that is a battle we ultimately lost. This story is a train wreck that will haunt your emotions, attack your values, and dement your very being.

But it is better than the original.

Combining the degrading rituals of action adventure and harlequin romance, we have succeeded in our venture. Some might call it misogynist, some might call it nonsensical, no one will call it quality, but fret not, for we promise your wasted money will find a good home.

In the wake of breaking even, all proceeds will be donated to charity. None of the money will be funneled back into the business empire that would use it to duplicate the very dreadfulness this story encompasses. Our best guess is that at least a million dollars was spent creating *Snakes on a Train,* the worst form of entertainment imaginable. That money had so many other more worthwhile places it could have gone, like breast surgery; like the sight of a woman's bosom slathered in salty wetness.

You want to talk about nobility, well, this is our chivalry; this is our knighting. Lay the sword upon us, for we are the good guys in all of this. Now allow us to stick the sword in you; to remove your chastity. Read further and receive your initiation; because we promise, when you have completed this story, you will certainly feel like you have been screwed.

PREPARE YOURSELF…

TO BE SNAKE-FUCKED IN HALF.

SNAKES ON A TRAIN

IN

CANADA

1

THE TRAIN STATION

Our story starts one fine summer afternoon in Winnipeg, a medium sized metropolitan city located at the geographical centre of Canada. Winnipeg is a nice city, all though it surely has its problems. Probably the largest problem in Winnipeg is that usually there is nothing much to do. Yet on this fine summer day in late August, the type of excitement left to only for the actors in Hollywood or and to the wildest of dreams, was about to show up in this most unlikely town.

While the first scene in this book takes place at the airport, this book is defiantly not about planes. No, too many stories start out that way. Airplanes are so old. Besides the endless stream of *Airport* films, many other titles have tried to capitalize on the utter helplessness that can overtake a situation when it is at 35, 000 feet.

Kurt Russell defeated a band of terrorists in *Executive Decision,* Harrison Ford did battle with…terrorists in *Air Force One*, and of course, Samual L. Jackson once got tired of a bunch of mother fucking snakes on a mother fucking plane in *Snakes on a Plane*. Those weren't terrorists; that was a terror-hiss.

This story is about a different mode of transportation. A mode that is more old-fashioned and more subdued than the fast-paced, commercially driven airport; a mode of transportation that brings us back to a time before televisions and Ipods; a time when only the thick, lush boreal forest existed for miles and miles and miles; a time when people like Gordon Lightfoot sang songs like *The Great Canadian Railroad Trilogy*, or something to that affect.

Of course, we are talking about the train.

There is only one train left in Canada that still transports people. After passenger airplanes arrived, promising to deliver people faster and for less money, most passenger trains simply stopped running. But one train, the VIA rail of Canada, still makes the routine trip across the great Canadian wilderness, chauffeuring those who wish to retreat back to a less-hurried time. Sporting 1960's style stainless steel railway cars with the distinguishable blue and yellow VIA insignia, the train has a sort of time-less nostalgia about it.

Most of the time, the train is nearly empty. The few people who do take the train are heading west, to the mountains. Very few people are heading east. What lies to the east are hundreds of kilometers of single lane railroad track and endless rocks and trees. The trip east, however, is stunning to experience – if you have a full 36 hours to spare. Most people don't have 36 hours to travel a distance you could drive in less than 24 and fly in under 2, and so the train is usually empty; silently making the pilgrimage back and forth across the harsh landscape on millions of dollars in government subsidies for a mere handful of people.

This particular day, at Union Station in downtown Winnipeg, crowds of people waited in line for the train. Not because they wanted to be there – but because they had no choice.

Earlier that day, a bomb-threat triggered a massive security shutdown of Winnipeg's International Airport. Tens of flights were cancelled, many more diverted to Saskatchewan. Inside the airport terminal, hundreds of security personnel, police and bomb sniffing dogs ran about, hurriedly trying to control the situation. A sniff from a bomb-detecting canine uncovered an actual bomb in an anonymously checked bag, and so for the time being the entire airport was in complete lockdown. Passengers had to wait hours to be released – many had to be strip-searched. Until the culprit was found, every single piece of evidence in the massive terminal building had to be combed through.

Some of the most lucky passengers immediately booked themselves a seat on the bus; others were able to put off their business and family reunions until the whole security mater could be resolved. Not everyone had this luxury, however, and many people found themselves in a pinch. One very fat and pompous business man who had been at the airport that day certainly did not have such luxury. He was on a very important business meeting – the outcome of which had dire consequences. The man was named Harry Taves, and to say the least, he wasn't happy about the whole ordeal.

"Sally! Get over here and tell this ASSHOLE that we need two tickets, RIGHT NOW!" Taves was talking to his assistant, Sally Knight. He was pointing his index finger at a very frazzled VIA rail employee, who hadn't experienced an angry mob of customers this size ever before.

"Yes sir, let me look after it, alright? You can go wait over there and grab a coffee," Sally was empathetic towards Taves, but that didn't mean she enjoyed it when he acted like an asshole in front of a group of people.

"Sorry about that," she apologized for Taves to the employee, "he is….well…. a little stressed out about work." Come to think of it, so was Sally. She had spent the last 48 hours of her life organizing one of the biggest business deals of her and Taves' career inside her blackberry universe. When she found out that the airport was closed, she knew there would be hell to pay.

"That's okay," the young man said, stumbling a bit over his words. How could he get upset when he was looking at a woman like Sally? Sally was probably one of the most attractive girls on the planet. She had blond hair coming down to her shoulders, soft delicate skin and small, trendy glasses. She was dressed in business casual attire, with a form fitting gray blouse and white shirt. Sally's best kept secret for her good looks was her diet of carrot juice and her vigorous work out routine. She also doesn't wear make-up, probably because she doesn't have to. Her eyes, especially, made her natural features sparkle in unison.

Sally blushed slightly, she thought the young man was cute.... but not her type. *What was her type*, Sally often wondered. Of course, Sally knew what her type was but she couldn't bring herself to think about it, for Sally was in love with a very special person – a person who probably didn't even know she existed. Maybe that would change one day. *And maybe Martians will invade Earth*, she thought to herself. "Two tickets for first class to Toronto, please."

The young man carefully entered all of the necessary information into his computer, and then produced two first class tickets. "Okay, you are in berth number sex.... oh! I mean six." The young man's Freudian slip made him now blush.

"Ha!" Sally laughed, "and I was really looking forward to room sex," she quipped.

"Ummm, well that could be arranged," the man mistook her comment as a come on.

"Oh! No thank you, creep!" And with that Sally turned from the desk.

"Rats, almost worked that time," the young man muttered softly to himself.

There were lots of other passengers gathering in the station. Many people were simply traveling out east to visit family and friends. Others were here hoping to make it to Toronto for business, just like Taves and Sally. From the comfort of the first class pre-boarding wait area, Sally eyed the many passengers who were gathering beside them. Her thoughts were drifting somewhere between work and pleasure, funny how those two things never end up being one and the same.

Taves interrupted her dreams suddenly.

"Fuck Sally, how many times do I have to tell you? One lump of sugar, not two! And for God Sakes, do up your shirt, you whore. Who are you trying to impress, anyways?" Taves certainly had a unique approach to talking to people. "What are you looking at, kid?" Taves was looking across the isle at a boy who had just overhead some pretty major profanity.

"Sir, don't you think you should quiet down a bit?" Sally offered a wise piece of advice. After all, this wasn't an airplane where people get off after a couple hours; this was a train to Toronto. If Taves annoyed someone, they would have to deal with it for 36 hours.

"FUCK! FUCK FUCK FUCK FUCK FUCK!" Taves was cranky, and when he was cranky he often started acting like a little kid. A little kid, that is, with a grown-up's mouth.

Sally sighed. *Soon enough this will be all over,* she thought. *We'll get to Toronto, make the deal, then have enough money to retire.* That was what she hoped. All of the time and energy she was investing for this business deal was on the assumption that she would get a cut of the profits. In the past, she had used her looks to charm Taves and get this job in the first place. Soon after being hired, she wondered if she had made a fatal mistake. She wondered what she might have to do for a cut of $20 million deal.

Across from the passenger waiting area, an equally attractive woman with dark features was beginning to prepare for the voyage. Cassandra Funk, as she is called, was the head stewardess on this voyage. Cassandra eyed the passengers, picking out the needy from the self-sufficient. Cassandra sighed as her eyes fell on Taves, his plump head and oblong features giving away his asshole characteristics. And when she overhead him talking to the blond woman beside him, her fears were only confirmed. Cassandra used her hands to tug at the waist of her uniform tunic. The dark blue uniform with matching blue pants was less then flattering on her, however her exceptional physique was still noticeable at a glance. Cassandra was feeling the burn already about today's voyage. *Crowds twice as large as usual*, she thought to herself, *looks like I'll be earning my money today*. The fact was, most of the time the VIA employees had it pretty easy. They were able to snooze and then do crossword puzzles all day if there were not many people on board. *Got to love this cushy government job*, she often thought to herself during those past voyages.

A whistle from above, followed by the low rumbling of an approaching train signaled the arrival of the VIA into the station. The train still needed to be cleaned and refueled, but it looked as if it was going to leave right on schedule today. The low rumble of the locomotive started to build, then slow. The high-pitched screech of the metal on metal breaks identified the train as slowing to a complete stop. VIA rail number 01, *The Canadian*, as it is affectionately called, had arrived in Winnipeg. Soon the passengers and crew would board the train and begin the journey east. No one expected this voyage to be very different from the norm. It was a nice, calm summers day...what could possibly go wrong?

***

"Looks like its gonna be a busy ride", sighed Cassandra. "VIA engineer 101, engineer 101, how are we doing up there?" Cassandra's radio cracked a few time, then the familiar voice of the engineer rattled back with the time honored response.

"VIA 101, checks are clear for boarding on my mark". Today's engineer was the veteran Casey McTavish. Casey had been on the job for over 30 years and knew how to run a tight ship. He hated running late, which was something the VIA did often enough on its own. But today, Casey felt good behind the controls of the lead locomotive. He was eager to load up the train and get it moving.

"Roger VIA engineer 101," Cassandra half rolled her eyes at what she considered the ridiculous lingo needed to operate the radios. In her mind, the ways of traveling by railroad were dying quickly. She was looking forward to finishing this voyage and taking a long holiday in Peru. And let me tell you something, she looks damn hot in a bathing suit.

"God dammed large ass country! Who decided to put this city here anywhos? God damn!" the voice of Taves was starting to annoy Cassandra, as well as the other crewmembers that were starting to assemble at the foot of the staircase that would lead passengers to the train platform.

"Gonna be a real long trip." Cassandra took one last deep breath and took out the radio again. "Passengers if I could have your attention please. VIA rail number 01 to Toronto will now begin boarding of first class. All those passengers holding first class tickets are asked to start heading towards the stairs. Thank you."

***

Meanwhile, on the other side of the globe from Winnipeg, a very different story was starting to unfold. High aloft in an office tower in downtown Shanghai, Janzo Kim – millionaire and eccentric all around bad-guy was wearily looking out of his 42nd floor window at the sprawling, polluted cityscape his building shadowed over.

Janzo Kim leaned back in his chair, his hands clenched together with his tan, pointy chin resting upon his two index fingers. He turned from the giant picture window and glared down at his employee who was standing before him in his dark oval office.

"What do you mean he's still going to Toronto? I thought we took care of that little problem?" Janzo Kim was a formidable character. His short, dark hair and pointed features translated into a ruthless personality.

"Yes sir, err, yes, well you see we didn't expect him to get on the t-ta-ta-train, sir," came the stuttery response of Kim's assistant, who looked down at the ground in disgrace. *I have failed my master*, he was thinking. *What price will I have to pay?* The assistant was supposed to get the bomb *onto* the plane, but somehow his intensions were thwarted by the Winnipeg Police.

"Idiot! What do I pay you for? You shit brain! That will be the last time you ever make a mistake! Take this!" And with a push of a button on the side of Kim's desk, a giant trap door opened underneath his assistant. The door swung down violently, revealing a pit full of rattlesnakes and cobras. "Say hello to my pit of snakes!"

There was a blood curdling scream and some blood splatter, then eerie silence. What was once a man was now a pile of rotting flesh. The unforgettable sounds of the snakes' hisses were all that remained.

"Get me another employee!" commanded Kim into his desk side microphone.

"Y-y-yes sir," came the all too knowing response of Kim's secretary who, from behind the thick oak doors to Kim's office, had heard everything.

"And call my limo.... it looks like I'll have to move to plan B", said Kim who suddenly seemed to have a new idea of how to stop Harry Taves from stealing his trinket empire.

2

SNAKES ON A TRAIN

14:58

Pinky Jordan sat crossed legged in the employee room behind the baggage carrousel in Winnipeg's Union station. At one point, employees wanting a smoke break used this room; but now, of course with the smoking ban in all public places, this was an empty and unused room. Pinky was on the phone with headquarters back in Langley.

"Dammit Rocko," shouted Pinky into the receiver, "all connecting flights have been cancelled to Toronto, this is our only chance." Special agent Pinky Jordan now waited for the response he was looking for. One of his hands was pressed the black cell phone against an ear, while another hand waved through his course brown hair.

"All right, all right!" was the impatient voice on the other end of the phone in Langley Virginia, CIA headquarters. It was the voice of Special agent in charge, Michael Rocko.

"Thank you! okay, let's do this!" Pinky was ecstatic. A couple hours ago when he found out that the airport was going to be completely shut down due to a bomb threat, he started to panic. *How far will they go to kill this guy?*

"Good luck then, agent Jordan, and good hunting!" the line went dead. By this time tomorrow Pinky would be in Toronto where he could finally solve one of the most deadly cases he had ever been on - a case involving a rouge agent and the Chinese government.

"Okay, let's do this and get 'er done!" thought Pinky. He put his jacket back on, covering his holster and badge. Pinky was sweating slightly, but he remained cool. His blue eyes darted across the room at this bag, which had something very important in it. Something very important indeed.

***

Janzo Kim closed the cover of his cell phone and sat back into the black leather seat of his company's limo. Kim hand an idea, but it was a risky one.

"Sir, are you sure about this?" was the response from the man on the other end of phone.

"You don't think I've exhausted all other options?" Kim had said back, impatiently.

"But sir, this is risky. This has never been done before... well almost never."

"It will work, it has to. It damn well has to." Janzo knew this was a risky plan. But he was all out of options at this point. Harry Taves had to die or that train had to never make it to Toronto.

"Okay, let's do it," commanded Kim into his cell phone. "Unleash the fury!"

***

A suspicious looking baggage handler stood beside the baggage car of VIA rail 01, *The Canadian.* A text message on his cell phone spelt out his orders. He was not to back down at this point.

His name was Kevin Hussein, an Iranian immigrant who came to Canada to start a new life. But the Harper government took away all of the social program he and his family relied on, and so just like so many other new families who are desperate for money and food, Hussein entered a life of crime. For Hussein, this was a big break. Some big wig in China had called him up personally for a unique mission. There was also a hefty paycheck waiting for him if he was successful.

"Just one more to load up," Hussein said to another VIA employee, busy loading passenger luggage into the car.

"Dang large one, eh?" the classic Canadian response came back from inside the car.

"Yes sir, special orders for this one, handle with extreme care it says."

"Okay, pass it up here." And with a grunt the two men lifted the large, white box into the train car. "Wow, what do you think is in here?" said the employee who bent down to look through one of the holes in the side of the box. Curiosity was about to kill the cat.

"Your mom!" Shouted Hussein. And with that a single gunshot echoed in the metal railway car. Hussein stood with a large gun in one hand; smoke leaking out of the barrel. "Have a fun voyage," he laughed as he took off his fake uniform revealing his Janzo Kim company jacket. "Snacks are located two cars back, HAHA!"

Murder. The worst of all sins – even in the eyes of Hussein. But how else was he going to pay his Hydro bill? Hussein knew his role in this world. He wasn't going to fail. Nothing could stop in his way now.

***

All of the passengers were now aboard the train. In coach, people began to settle into their seats for the long voyage. In the sleeper cars, families began to unpack their suitcases and check out their cots. In the diner car and bar car, employees began to get ready for the rush of hungry and thirsty passengers.

"All aboard!" Shouted Guss. Guss was the conductor aboard this voyage. He really only had two jobs: say "all aboard" and take tickets from the passengers. This allowed Guss to get drunk before most voyages because he usually didn't have to talk to anyone.

As if on cue, the train lurched forward a few inches, then slowly the huge metal cars began to follow the locomotive out of the station. A high-pitched whistle from the locomotive signaled its departure from Union Station. *36 Hours to Toronto.*

3

EXCESS BAGGAGE

15:20

The long, narrow passenger train quickly picked up speed as it left Union Station in downtown Winnipeg. The downtown environment quickly gave way to the extensive suburban sprawl and then finally to flat, golden prairie. The sun was starting to hang low on the horizon as the afternoon slowly started to give way to early evening.

Today's VIA train was eight railway cars long – the baggage car scouted up front, followed by the two coach cars, the bar car with the scenic dome attachment, the diner car, the two first class sleeper cars, and finally the luxurious observation car with the panoramic dome attachment as well as another first class bar. Although the train is old, its comforts and style still make for an exceptional journey. One of the best features of the VIA rail, however, is its team of staff – handpicked members of the bilingual elite trained to offer exceptional customer service. The staff are encouraged to mingle with the passengers, which often leads to a few hook-ups now and again.

Inside the bar car, the fourth car back behind the locomotive, the head bartender, Stephanie Warlock, was busy opening the bar up for business. Stephanie bent over to grab a Moslen Canadian from the bottom of the bar fridge. Stephanie was serving her new regular, Jack Baytel, a French Canadian business man who was making his routine voyage back to Toronto after another business meeting. Jack, who was making his thirteenth consecutive voyage across the Canadian landscape, had a terrible fear of flying and so relied heavily on the train to get him to where he needed to go. Jack was now eyeing Stephanie's flawless body, her subtle perfume sending him into a fantastic day dream.

"One Moslen Canadian, Jack," replied the soft, sexy voice of Stephanie Warlock, recent university graduate and aspiring model.

"Oh, yes thank you Steph," croaked Jack, who was brought back to the present suddenly from his Harlequin type sex scene in his mind.

"What were you looking at, Jack," questioned Steph who had noticed Jack starring at her more and more the past few voyages.

"Steph, you are a nice girl. And, well, I'm just interested in you," Jack had thought long and hard about this moment, when he would finally tell Steph the truth about how he felt. But unfortunately, those were not the words he had though long and hard about. In fact, it seemed to be the beer that was doing most of the talking for him.

"Oh Jack! What would your husband think!" quipped Steph, who knew of Jack's gay marriage. Steph actually really like Jack, but she knew him too well at this point. Steph had a rule, never date gay men. She found that all of her gay relationships turned out bad in the end, usually involving a harsh breakup.

"He doesn't have to know," responded Jack in a cool, quiet voice. The truth was, Jack wanted Stephanie more then Markus, and even more then Jesus. His bisexual nature was finally starting to break the surface. Jack hoped that this voyage would finally break the spell and let him have the sex he always wanted. A few more beers, and maybe it would all come true.

"I'll have another, Steph," and with that, Jack was once again lost in dream as Steph bent over to grab another cold one from the bar car fridge.

***

"Mommy, can I have an ice cream?"

The mommy was frustrated as it was, and the last thing she needed was for her clumsy son to drop another ice cream cone all over the floor and embarrass her in front of a bunch of strangers. But her little boy was so precious to her that she could never say no.

The mommy was leading her little boy through the dome car, on the way back to their sleeping compartment where her husband was waiting for them. Of course, "husband" was a loose term. Truth be told, they barely spoke anymore. Their marriage was for the sake of their son, nothing more. Her husband was cheating on her, and she damn well knew it. It became pretty obvious the day she came home and found a pair of panties in the couch cushions with the word "mistress" written in black lettering on them.

She was never in a hurry to get back to her husband, so the mommy figured a quick stop to get ice cream couldn't hurt.

The little boy chose mint chocolate chip, and he began devouring into the cone in his usual careless fashion the second it was handed to him. *I'll be on my hands and knees cleaning up another mess anytime now* the mommy thought to herself.

As the two of them began walking again, the mommy couldn't help but notice a couple of shadowy figures enter into the dome car. She couldn't make out their faces, but they looked pretty shady to her. There was just something off about them. Something mysterious. She hoped that she wouldn't have to see them again for the rest of the trip.

***

The two shadowy figures the mommy saw were deep in secretive conversation.

"So you spoke to the boss, eh?" whispered one of the dark figures to the other.

"Yes, and all is good now. We get off at Timsons Point, four hours from now," answered the second shadowy man. He then took out his cell phone and read the text message that had suddenly appeared.

"What, what is it now?" the first man wanted to know. He was uneasy, and probably drawing un-necessary attention to their secret meeting in the dome car.

"Oh that, nothing, don't worry about it," replied the second man, who was quick to change the subject. "Now, you know what to do."

"Yes, yes I do. I will go now and prepare myself."

"Good, and in three hours, let us meet again to discuss plan B, just in case we need it," the second dark man was a fan of over planning. A bad experience back in Reno had drilled the need for a back up plan into him long ago.

"These people won't know what hit 'em!" said the first man, a bit too loud this time. An elderly man looked over at that remark, showing some signs of concern over the sentence he thought he just heard.

"Yes, these people don't know how beautiful this voyage is, my Canadian friend" *and complete idiot*, thought the second man who tried to make the other man's sentence sound benign to the old man. *We must leave now and prepare*, he thought, *I must get ready for what will surely be the most difficult mission in my entire life*. And with that, the two men receded back down the stairs and disappeared in two separate directions.

***

Jack had his hands in his pocket. Stephanie noticed this, but opted not to mention it, despite the immense strangeness inherent in a man sitting on a bar stool in such a fashion.

She handed him another shot of vodka and he downed it in one swift swig, without so much as moving his other hand from its unusual location.

Indeed, Stephanie liked Jack, but there was no questioning it – the guy was kind of strange.

"Well Steph, I guess I'll talk to you a little later. I think I'm going to go lie down for a little while." Jack rose and shoved the shot glass back at Stephanie. He threw a fifty-dollar bill at her and turned to walk away.

"I'll miss you," she responded smugly. Stephanie pocketed the money and began wiping down the counter.

Her next customer arrived almost immediately. The man took a seat where Jack had been sitting only seconds before. He ordered a whiskey, looking somewhat apprehensive, even a bit mysterious. That's what Stephanie thought, anyway.

The man was sporting a suit and tie, and had the very typical businessman look to him. *Another one* she thought. She dealt with his type all the time, but it was rare when one she had never seen before came and drank during the trip. She had her ten or twelve regulars, and that was it. VIA rail 01 was infamous for businessmen making quick commutes between Winnipeg and the nation's capital, and pretty much all of them wanted in her pants.

Stephanie could admit it to herself – she was an attractive woman. The problem was, she didn't find businessmen attractive in the least. In fact she subconsciously disliked them. "Business" itself was such a shallow concept to Stephanie, part of the reason why she took the job she did. Being a bartender was one of the least political jobs she could think of. Or at least that she was qualified for.

Luckily, she was also a realist. Stephanie needed money, and lots of it. She had a daughter at home to feed, and horny drunk businessmen provided good tips; just another example of their extreme superficiality.

"And how are you today, sir?" Stephanie finally asked the man after a long pause.

"Fine, thanks," replied the man, who was clearly uneasy about something. Sweat was pouring from his brow, and his hands were trembling as he sipped his whiskey.

Even still, there was something kind of off about the man. Something shadowy. Something mysterious.

Yep, it was going to be a long night.

***

Cassandra Funk needed some time alone. The passengers in coach were complaining as usual.

"I want a blanket...." One would say.

"I want some water..." another would follow.

"I want a magazine, stewardess, another magazine....hellllllooooooo, today missy."

Enough was enough. Cassandra retreated to the front of the train. The baggage car was a darker then the rest of the train. It was also a lot cooler. The cold temperature was exactly what Cassandra needed right now. That and a good drink. But as Cassandra reached into her inside breast pocket to grab her flask, the train jigged and reeled from side to side, sending her off balance. Cassandra fell hard, right on top of a giant white container near the rear of the baggage car.

"Shit!" yelled Cassandra in surprise. She usually didn't loose her balance. Maybe this was a sign that she was getting tired. "Soon I'll retire from this tin box and become an actress, like I always dreamed." Then, out of the corner of her eye, Cassandra saw a dark figure move near the rear of the baggage car. She replaced the lid that had been dislodged from the white container she fell on, and yelled out, "who's there?" She was met by silence. "I said, who is there, show yourself! I know Kung Fu!"

"Okay, okay, please lady! Don't shoot! It is just me, a humble hobo who is hitching a ride! But please, lady don't kick me off. My mama, she is sick in Toronto and I need to get there to be by her side. Please, kind lady, don't kick me off. I have but no money, but I will do anything for my passage. Anything!"

Damn hobos, thought Cassandra. *But maybe this could work out well.*

"Okay hobo, I have something for you to do. Come here!" The hobo slowly revealed himself from the shadows. He was handsome, but obviously lacked some personal hygiene.

"Yes, please lady anything. But don't throw me off this train. The beavers and wolves will surely eat me alive!" Cassandra knew she couldn't throw this man off the train. It would be cruel subjecting someone to the

Canadian wild this time of year. A man wouldn't last one day before being devoured by the angry moose. If the moose missed, then surely the bear or the wolf would catch him. The mighty beaver would quickly trap him, and before he could escape, slap! Beaver time.

"Yes come here at once, let me see you!" Cassandra really did know Kung Fu, and so was not scared of this hobo. "Give me your hand."

"But lady, my hand, I need my hand to live. I am an artist, you see! Please, oh lady have mercy!" The hobo was scared now.

"COME HERE!" Cassandra commanded. "Now, give me your hand!" The hobo reached out, eyes closed, anticipating the worse. How could he have been so stupid! Now his hand, the only thing that supplemented his income, was about to be lost forever.

"Please, be quick", the hobo whimpered.

"Now put your hand here….. yes….. that's right….. ooooh….. that's good." Cassandra moved the man's hand down, slowly, until his hand was right where she wanted it. "Good, just like that, yes! Yes!"

"Oh god!" The hobo knew his hand was lost forever. No longer would its virgin fingers be the same. Oh the agony!

4

THE LOCOMATIVE

15:48

Far from the hobo's desperate cries, Casey McTavish, the lone engineer and ONLY PERSON ABLE TO DRIVE THE TRAIN sat with his eyes focused on the track that lay ahead. *This was the long stretch*, Casey knew. The track between Kewatin and Elmer's Sound was long, straight and quiet. Little radio contact and little to do. It was this point in the voyage that McTavish had to fight the hardest to stay awake. The gentle hum of the diesel motor was relaxing; however it was also hiding a more alarming sound, a sound that was slowly creeping up behind Casey.

The old diesel locomotive not only had to propel the heavy eight-car passenger train forward, it also had to supply the electrical power for all of the train's modern day amenities, like the air-conditioning, the stoves in the kitchen and the televisions in the bar car.

I wonder if Cassandra thinks I'm hot, wondered Casey. "Naw, I'm out of her league," he reminded himself aloud. But the truth was that Casey hadn't been with a woman since Joan, his loving railway companion that stayed in the caboose, until that fateful July day in 1958. Casey remembered that day all too well. The day the caboose fell behind.

"Never go after a fallen railway car," Casey remembered the voice of his instructor back in train school. "You never know what dangers lie in the Canadian Wilderness. Just let 'er go, that is the best advice I can give you. Let 'er go." And so Casey let her go, poor Joan trapped in the Caboose in the middle of the wild. Alone, scared and crying for help.

A jig from the train as it passed a corner awoke Casey from his day dream. *Poor Joan,* thought Casey, *I shouldn't have left you behind.* But that was long ago. A much larger problem was about to plague Casey's thoughts. If only Casey's left ear wasn't damaged from years of demolition work. Maybe then he could hear danger approaching from behind.

***

Far from the noise of the locomotive, the first class passengers were busy settling into their small but comfortable sleeping compartments. Each sleeping berth had its own toilet and sink, as well as single or double bunk beds for either couples or families. Inside one these sleeping compartment, Harry Taves had fallen as sleep and was snoring loudly.

He had finally fallen asleep ten minutes ago, and Sally couldn't have been more relieved. She was used to putting up with his bullshit, but every once in a while it got to be too much, and she needed a break.

As long as she had one, she decided to make the best of it. She went to the bar car to see if the rumours were true.

The thing was, Sally was in love. In love with the most unlikely of people. And when the fact that her and her boss would be traveling on the VIA train on that night, her heart started beating just a little faster. The odds were astronomical, but Sally believed in fate, and she truly felt that fate might be dealing her a decent hand on this night. Could it be possible? Would she be there?

Sally stepped into the bar car with her eyes closed. She was almost nervous. She wanted so bad for it to be true. Slowly she opened her eyes.

And there she was.

She was standing there, so beautiful, so perfect. It was actually happening. She couldn't believe it. Her dream girl was actually there, pouring drinks.

Stephanie Warlock was talking to a man, a man who looked...mysterious. Yes, that was it. That was the only word Sally could think to describe him. But who cared about that. Stephanie was working on this train. Stephanie was a mere ten feet away from her. *There is a God* Sally thought.

***

Next to the bar car was the coach car. Seating about fifty passengers in rows of blue-suede seating, the coach car was designed for comfort and efficiency. Some of the seats even flipped around to face backwards, ideal for a group of four or a small family. Sitting next to the window was Pinky Jordan, the lone CIA agent aboard the train.

Pinky open his cell phone again, a new text message awaited. *Damn CIA, always paranoid*, though Pinky. The message read as follows:

"Agent Jordan, please confirm intensions. Do you believe hostile is on board. Over."

But Pinky wasn't able to respond to this message because interference from the vast Canadian shield was blocking his reception. *Damn Canadian shield*, cursed Pinky to himself. But it was true, enemy hostiles were aboard. Half and hour ago, Pinky decided to engage in plan B. He hated going to the back-up plan so soon without contacting headquarters, but without reception Pinky needed to rely on his instincts as an experienced CIA agent.

Pinky got out of his seat in coach and started to saunter towards the diner car. On his way, he passed a middle aged woman yielding a small child. *Wowzers, though Pinky, check out the rack on that!* Pinky was noticing the firm, voluptuous breasts of Mrs. Patterson, the woman who occupied one of the sleeping berths aboard this voyage. Careful not to stare, Pinky averted his eyes just in time to avoid an equally sensual stare from Mrs. Patterson.

Vicky Patterson was immediately attracted to the strange man's crotch as Pinky squeezed by her in the corridor. *Wowzers, thought Vicky, look at the buldge on that one!* Indeed it was true, years of hard combat service in the United States Marines that turned Pinky into an attractive, buldgy man. *I want some of that for dessert,* quipped Vicky to herself, who was suddenly starting to enjoy the fact that there were still twenty-nine hours until Toronto. *Plenty of time for a little fun.*

Pinky passed through the double doors into the diner car. Inside, the view was spectacular. Dressed in pink drapes and white marble was the luxurious VIA rail diner car. Everything about this car described a by gone era of luxury and excess. Even though the car was a little run down, the overall feeling of luxury still emanated from the walls.

"Good day, sir," came the voice of the waiter. "Please, have a seat here." He beckoned towards a table in the far corner. "Shall I start you off with a coffee, sir?"

"Please," said Pinky. "Double double. Oh, and a Boston cream too."

"Very good, sir." A coffee and donut was all Pinky needed right now to gather his thoughts. Only four more hours left, judging by his watch, before the real test of his training as a CIA agent would come into play.

***

Casey was concentrating on the track ahead when a terrible pain suddenly caught him off guard. It felt like a million little needles were suddenly shooting up his body. Looking down, Casey saw the horrific, jaw dropping reason for the excruciating pain. A snake, about one metre long with huge fangs and green scales was chomping on his man-sword.

"Shit! There's a snake on my dick!" cried Casey as he violently swung back and forth in the cabin of the locomotive. Outside, the wild Canadian landscape flew by at a dizzyingly fast rate. "Get off my dick you fucking snake!"

hisssssssssssssss hissssssssssssssssssss was all that the snake said in return.

"Ahhh, fuck! My dick! My dick! My diiiiiiickkkkk!" and before the snake had finished swallowing the foreskin, Casey McTavish, engineer of VIA rail 01 and the only person aboard licensed to drive the train dropped dead on the floor of his locomotive. Casey's last thoughts were of his lovely Joan. *I'm coming up now, I'll see you soon my lovely.*

The passengers and crew of VIA rail 01, destined for Toronto Canada, were now in real danger. How long would it be before the train would crash, or loose control and fly off the rails? Unbeknownst to the rest of the train, but knownst to us, things were about to get much, much worse.

5

SEX ON A TRAIN

16:01

Cassandra lifted her head, and sucked in some of the cool, fresh air that surrounded the baggage compartment area. Beneath her, the young hobo lay gasping for air. Cassandra's uniform was half off, revealing her voluptuous body. Sweat glistened across her body, highlighting her figure in the dim light.

"Can...can I go now?" whimpered the hobo, who had figured he had done his bid for a free ticket.

"Not....yet...." gasped Cassandra, who was having far too much fun to let him go just yet. "On your knees, boy."

"Oh please, no more.... I can't take any more!"

"Shut up, fool. Do as I say. And remember, this is our little secret!" Cassandra had a way of controlling the weaker sex to do her bidding. "Now! On your knees, bitch!"

The hobo got up onto his knees. "Like this?" he whimpered softly.

"Good, now... again! Start again!" Cassandra laughed and flung herself upon the hobo. And for the second time, Cassandra and the strange hobo man engaged in awkward train sex on top of people's personal luggage. It was awesome.

***

Stephanie sighed. She had just finished a long shift behind the counter and was ready for some R and R. She placed the "Back in one hour" sign on top of the countertop and got up to leave. Her destination: her employee berth located two cars back.

"One more before I go, sugar?" asked Stephanie to the attractive young woman who had been sitting at the bar for the past fifteen minutes.

"Hit me one more time, Steph," said Sally, who needed a confidence drink. The past fifteen minutes had been agonizing for her, as all she wanted was to rip her cloths off and smother herself with Stephanie Wardlock.

"Okay, one more then I have to leave for my break," said Steph, who was curious why this young lady seemed so interested in her. The woman was asking so many questions like, "so, do you have a boyfriend," and "do you like movies that are about female jails?"

"Thanks…say, mind if I join you on your break? I could use the company," said Sally, who was feeling some confidence drifting inside of her. Oh how she was aching for some girl on girl action.

Stephanie thought about that for a second, and then said, "well, why not. You like scrabble, sugar?"

"Hell yes, I love scrabble"

"Really, me too, one of my favorite games"

Sally was too excited, "I once spelt lesbian on a triple letter score and got fifty bonus points for using all of my letters."

"Well I once spelt clitoris by using a blank, and the 'T' continued on to spell 'thrusting'. I think I got 200 points for that word." Steph was extending the challenge. However, Sally was reading into this a little differently.

She wants me! I know it. Just play it cool, Sally, thought Sally to herself.

"Okay then, lets go play," said Steph, as she placed the "back in one hour sign" on the counter. The two very attractive girls left the car together and headed down the train to the employee berths. Let me tell you, this story is about to get really hot.

***

Pinky put down his coffee mug and starred out the window. He shivered at the sight of millions of acres of untamed wilderness. *Why would anyone live up here, anyways?* A figure suddenly appeared from his peripheral vision and sat down beside him at the fancy dining car table.

"Hi there, mind if I join you?" It was the female voice of Mrs. Patterson, the woman Pinky had brushed past in the corridor just a few minutes ago.

"Not at all, its nice to you meet you, miss?"

"Patterson, but please, call me Vicky."

"Vicky, what a nice name," cooed Pinky. It had been a while since Pinky was with a woman. And this woman seemed to help ground agent Jordan who was feeling nervous after his last communicate with headquarters.

"Why, is that a gun in your pocket, or are you just glad to see me?" said Vicky in return, a thin smile pursed her red lips. Vicky was an attractive woman, but sometimes she forgot that she could use her looks to woo men. Years of unhappy marriage sometimes left Vicky feeling trapped and ugly. But right now, she was more alive then ever. The bold, strong figure sitting before her obvious took good care of his body, too. And by the look of it, he was also well equipped.

"Oh! You mean this?" Pinky turned crimson, ashamed that Vicky saw it. "Sorry, I thought it was well hidden.... I, don't usually..." Pinky was interrupted by Vicky.

"That's okay, I like it, really. Does it have a name?" Pinky was surprised at the comment. *A name?*

"Well, I like to call it my little magnum," said Pinky in honest response. It was years since he called it that, but back in cadet school Pinky's magnum was known as being one of the hardest to beat.

"Do you think I could see it, perhaps later, in private, of course," asked Vicky, who saw her chance to take this conversation to the next level.

"Sure, I'd be happy to, how about right now?" Vicky could almost scream with delight.

"I know just the place, following me!" Vicky led Pinky down the halls of the long train until they reached a room marked "Do not enter"

"I don't know. Vicky, should I really bust out my magnum in that room? What if someone walks in on us?"

"Relax, I have a key!" Vicky blushed with excitement. *He is a little strange for naming it that*, thought Vicky, *but who cares, he is damn hot!*

"Wow, where did you get that?" asked Pinky. *Always so quick to interrogate*, he thought to himself. The characteristic that made Pinky so good for the CIA sometimes made him socially awkward.

"I stole it from the conductor!" she quipped. "That drunkard has been asleep ever since we left

Winnipeg!" Pinky liked this woman even more now, she was risky and dangerous.

"Okay, quick before someone sees us!" Pinky was excited to show Vicky his little toy. The two adults entered the room and locked the latch behind them. Inside were some breaker panels, a mop bucket and several porno mags on the floor.

"Man, that conductor is a real pig!" thought Vicky aloud. "Now, lets see it, mister! Show me what you've got."

Pinky reached down to his belt and undid his holster, revealing his shiny, silver fire-arm. "Pretty cool, eh? Standard issue in the CIA."

Vicky couldn't have been more disappointed.

6

OUT OF CONTROL

16:22

It was still dark in Shanghai; the sun had no yet risen. Outside the congested cityscape, our dark, evil villain was preparing to leave China for the wide open wilderness of Canada.

Janzo Kim was at the airport in Shanghai. His secretary scuttled behind him as he hurriedly made his way through the airport towards his private suite. Kim, a multibillionaire, landed his first business deal in this airport. He remembered that day quite clearly. The nervous energy that flowed through him, the feeling of adrenaline pumping in his blood. That was how he was feeling now, except his time he was preparing to prevent a major business deal. *Why did it have to be a son?* Kim had wondered for so many years. His eldest son, Chi, had always been a rebel. *Always had to do things differently, always had to go against the grain.* Kim had once thought that Chi must have had some sort of mental disability. *Always laughing, always having fun,* was how Kim remembered Chi as a boy. *But work isn't fun, it can't be fun.* Kim's philosophy on work didn't rub off on Chi the way he hoped. And now here he was, in his private airport suite preparing to board his private 747 jumbo jet to finally set things right. *Finally, I can fix all of the mistakes I made bringing that child into this world.*

"Sir, I've just got off the phone with the pilot. We'll be departing within the hour." Kim's trustworthy secretary interrupted his vengeful thoughts.

"Good, and thank you for your help," came the sincere response. *I am not a bad man, but sometimes even good men have to do bad things.*

"Good luck," was the equally sincere response of Saki Kim, Janzo's trusted secretary and secret lover. *Good luck father, I will miss you dearly...*

***

Aboard VIA rail 01, no one had noticed that the train's engineer, Casey McTavish was lying dead in his locomotive. During the long stretch between stations, it was sometime common to not hear any radio communication from the train's engineer. But back in Winnipeg, up in the high tech railway control room in

Union Station, one man had noticed. And little did this lone watchman know that he would soon become tangled up in the most daring rescue operation every performed on earth.

"Sir, I think we have a problem here," sounded a young man dressed in shirt and tie. He was looking at a red blip on a giant screen that mapped out the entire railroad network in northern Ontario.

"What is it, Shamus?" answered the duty manager. Problems were rare, and when they did happen it was usually because of a small electrical problem.

"VIA 01 failed to stop at Junction 462. I gave him a red light, but he just kept going." Said Shamus to the on-duty station manager.

"You sure this isn't an electrical problem again?" asked the duty manager, who didn't want a repeat of what happened two months ago, when the entire railroad network had to be shut down because of a computer virus. He was almost fired that day because of the estimated $5 million the rail companies lost from being late in delivering their freight.

"Sir, I don't think this is an electrical problem. I'm reading other traffic clearly on my tele-viewer," Shamus was clearly getting more and more worried as the time ticked by.

"Okay, lets just be safe then," sighed the manager. "Clear that rail line and give that train some room. Let's try the radios" Using the radio was difficult, because the interference from the Canadian shield reflected much of the beam.

"VIA rail engineer 01 this is mission control, do you read?" Shamus was met by dull static on the other end.

"VIA rail 01, do you read?" No response. "Nothing sir."

"Keep trying, Shamus, I'm going to sound the alarm." The duty manager took a deep breath and picked up a red phone on the desk. "We've got an emergency here," he said to the dull voice on the other end of the receiver. "VIA rail 01 is out of control. Repeat, VIA rail 01 is out of control."

***

Stephanie Warlock was deep in concentration. One wrong move at this point, and she would loose. The game had been so close up until this point; her opponent was a worthy adversary.

"Ok, I have one," said Stephanie. "B-U-T-T-O-C-K, let's see that's... one-two-five-eleven-..... twenty-seven points!" Stephanie let out a smile. That was a good score this late in the game.

Sally was also looking for a good score, if you know what I mean. Sally looked at the word, and then she had an idea. "Challenge!" She shouted the command someone uses when they think the word played in a game of Scrabble is not one that can be found in the official Scrabble players dictionary.

"What? Buttock is a real word!" Steph was surprised. Up until this point, Sally seemed to be well aware of how the game worked. Could this be the mistake of an amateur?

"Nope, I definitely challenge. Prove that buttocks is a real word!" Sally pursed her lips together and leaned into towards Stephanie. "What does it mean, then?"

"You know... it means... your butt, your ass, you know, your rump!" Stephanie still didn't get why Sally was having trouble with this word.

"Show me, I still don't understand," Sally's blue eyes sparkled, as she used her fingers to draw her hair back behind her left ear, the tell tail sign of someone flirting. The skin goes a deep crimson and the lips begin to moisten. Sally was in love.

"Gee-wiz sugar, you still don't know what I mean? Here, I'll show you," Stephanie stood up and took off her pants.

"Nope, still don't get it," cooed Sally. *Wow, what a buttock!*

"Oh come on, girl! Here, give me your hand. THIS, I MEAN THIS!" Stephanie placed Sally's hand on her buttock. A warm current of electricity then passed from Sally into Stephanie. The electricity momentarily stunned Steph, but then everything became crystal clear. This was the best game of scrabble ever.

***

Cassandra got off of the limp, broken body of the hobo. His eyes were blood shot, and a mixture of sweat and blood covered his face. *Last time he tries to ride free*, thought Cassandra to herself. "Hey you, get up! Get up I say!" But the limp body of the hobo didn't move. *Men*, though Cassandra, *always fall right asleep*. But when Cassandra tried to shake the hobo awake, he still didn't move. "Shit!" Cassandra cursed. "He's dead?!" *How is this possible?* Then she remembered the loud snap that she heard after her ninth orgasm. She thought it was the luggage creaking underneath them, but it seemed to be the man's spine breaking in two. Unsure of what to do, Cassandra panicked and opened the lid to the giant white container she had fallen on top of when she first stepped into the baggage car. *I must act quickly, before someone sees me!* Cassandra lifted the limp body and put it into the container. *Funny*, thought Cassandra, *it sounds like the gas pipes are leaking slowly... owell no time for that*. The body fit well inside the box, but it was too full to put the lid on properly. A sound coming from behind made Cassandra jump. She quickly put the lid half way on and turned, just in time to see the conductor stumble through the door.

"Oh, hi Guss," said Cassandra, using her sleeve to wipe off the sweat on her brow.

"Mudda fudka, yousravl alwe," the incoherent ramblings of the drunkard conductor relieved Cassandra slightly.

"Okay, Guss, what ever you say!" Cassandra didn't waste any time leaving the baggage car. *Phew, its just that drunkard conductor!*

Guss took out a bottle from his secret stash and took a big swig. "Fudda buckin fucdga mocka eledpdadla.... SNAKE! OH SHIT SNAKE, SNAKE, SNAKE! OH PLEASE HELP ME!," Guss' first and last coherent sentence of his life passed by un-noticed as a giant green snake ferociously bit Guss in the face. Blood splattered everywhere. Guss' last fight for his life resulted in a horrific display of blood and guts smeared all over the floor and ceiling, as well as all over everyone's luggage. The snakes were now loose on an out of control train in the middle of the Canadian wilderness. It was only a matter of time before complete annihilation and death.

7

CONSPIRACY THEORY

16:45

Harry Taves awoke suddenly. For a second, he forgot where he was. The shock of waking up in an unfamiliar environment brought him quickly back to the present. He was on a train, *Fuck*, he cursed to himself, *are we there yet?* Outside, the landscape passed by steadily, the gentle clickity clack of his railcar oscillating everything slightly from side to side. "Sally! Sally! Where are you, Sally?" Taves has a real grump after naps. His patience was especially thin. "God damn it girl, where are you?" But Tave's cries for his assistant had to go unanswered for now; Sally was a little preoccupied at the moment, if you know what I mean.

After slashing some water on his face, Taves was ready to walk about the train to find something to occupy his time with. He looked in the mirror. *You're a good looking guy, Harry.* But he wasn't that good lucking at all. An accident when he was a baby made his head look too triangular. His diet of coca-cola and beer nuts had left him with a sizable gut. His fine, white hairs were starting to recede, and his nose was two sizes too large. The truth was that Harry had a crush on his assistant. The only reason he hired her was because Sally used to flirt with him. But now, any chance of a romantic reunion between the two of them was gone. From Sally's perspective, there was never anything there in the first place. She was only after his money, which he defiantly had lots of.

Harry Tave's began to make the big bucks after signing a deal with the manufacturer of Kinder Surprise to provide the little toys that go inside the chocolate shells. He then invested some money and got lucky at a few horse races. But the business deal he was going to make in Toronto would outscore everything to date. Chi Kim was about to offer Tave's a permanent slice of the Kim family trinket pie. The deal would provide Tave's with enough trinkets to form a small army, and enough cash to actually buy a small army. *But where is Sally?* Tave's was not worried, Sally was a loyal assistant. Tave's opened the door to his sleeping berth and started down the long, skinny corridor to the bar car. "I could use a little drink to lift my spirits," he thought aloud.

At the bar car, Tave's found a sign that read "Back in one hour" on the counter. "Fuck me!" Shouted

Tave's. A young boy playing his Nintendo looked up at the outburst.

"Gee Wiz mister, you shouldn't be cursing like that!" The young boy had balls talking to Tave's like that.

"Kid, go to hell," retorted Tave's.

"I'm telling!" threatened the kid.

"Here, buy yourself something nice," said Tave's as he handed the kid a five-dollar bill. *That should shut him up.* But it didn't.

"No way mister, a world like that is gonna cost you more then five bucks."

"Oh for fuck sakes! Here!" Tave's wanted the kid out of his face. "That's all I've got on me, okay? Is that enough you little twerp?" He handed the kid his wallet which had an Amex Card, a driver's license and about $300 dollars (Canadian) in fifty and twenty dollar denominations.

"Holly shit!" shouted the young boy.

"Ah Hah! Got you, you just swore, now give me back my money and fuck off!" Tave's loved to play games, when he could win of course. "Before I tell your mommy what you just said to me!"

"No please mister, don't tell her, I'll do anything!" the boy pleaded. He would be grounded for sure.

"It'll cost you!" said Taves. Business was business, whether it was a trinket market mogul or an eight year old boy.

"I don't have any money, though!"

"Well what's that you got there?" said Tave's, pointing towards the Nintendo.

"Oh man! That's my Nintendo, mister. You can't have that!"

"Okay, but I'm going to find your mommy and tell on...."

"Okay okay!" the boy didn't want to hear the rest of that sentence. "Here, take it."

Tave's now had something to occupy his time with. *Its like taking candy from a baby!* He went behind the bar counter and helped himself to a beer, then stumbled back to his sleeping berth. The little boy wished that the evil man would drop dead. Who knows, maybe he'll get his wish sometime soon.

***

Just upstairs from the bar, another man sat watching the scenery pass by. The man kept looking at his watch, nervously awaiting something. The dome car offered the man some more space to breathe – the tight compartments of the metal train seemed like they were closing in on him from all side.

"Nervous?" An elderly voice broke the still silence.

Had I said something aloud, the man thought to himself. *Was this guy on to me?*

"I know how you feel, believe me," continued the old man. His tired eyes focusing on the shadowy, dark figure sitting across form him. "The name's Peter," he extended his hand in greeting.

Should I use my real name? Thought the younger man. He figured this guy was of no real threat. "I-I am Kevin Hussein," he said softly.

"Kevin, nice to meet you young man. Now tell, what are you nervous about?"

This guy was defiantly on to him, but how? Why? "I-I-don't know what you mean, old man."

"Ha Ha! Oh boy, it is pretty obvious!"

It was?

"You don't like the train, don't you?" the old man questioned further.

A wave of relief flowed through Kevin Hussein. "Yes, oh, yes it is true, I have a fear of trains. Its silly, I know, but I really do hate them."

"Well now boy, its not silly," a wise grin formed on the mouth of the old man. "I was once scared myself. But then I hated all them dang terrorists flying around up there," he pointed towards the sky, then continued, "so I started taking the train, and now I'm over my fear."

Terrorists? Hussein was stunned by the remark. *This old man was on to him,* he could feel it.

"Now don't worry," the old man could sense his comment wasn't helping ease Kevin's apprehension. "I won't tell anyone."

You better not, or I'll slice your throat! Thought Kevin to himself. He opened up his cell phone and sent a short text message to his partner.

"Now, I have a little trick that can help." The old man got out of his seat and leaned in close to Hussein. "You need to take your socks off!" The old man revealed his bare feet to Hussein. "You see! Ha Ha, works like a charm, trust me!"

"Um.... Okay..." Kevin Hussein wasn't sure what to make of this old man. *Friendly or foe? Crazy or just pretending to be crazy?*

"Go on, try it!" The old man let out a deep belly laugh and gestured towards Hussein's feet.

"Might as well, I guess," said Kevin, not wanting to draw more awkward attention. He bent down and took off his brown leather shoes and white, ankle-high shocks.

"Hey, it works! Son of a bitch, it works!" shouted Kevin Hussein after stripping his shoes and socks.

"Good luck, kid," the old man said, as he turned to leave the dome car. "And remember, we're all in this together."

What the hell did that mean. Kevin Hussein wasn't sure what this guy knew, but he was pretty sure he'd better eliminate the possibility of being found out. He reached into his jacket pocket and felt the cold, steely grip of his revolver. He sent one last text message to his partner, and then turned to follow the old man.

***

Pinky Jordan wiped the lipstick from his mouth. He was starring into the bathroom mirror, the fluorescent light accentuating every line and wrinkle in on his face. He had just had a massive orgasm, and it was awesome.

It started out perfectly normal; the blond haired woman came and sat next to him in the diner car. The next thing he knew, he was showing her his pistol. And now, here he was, wiping the red lipstick off his face. It happened so fast, he wasn't even sure it happened at all. After all, it had been such a long time...

Then agent Jordan's cell phone vibrated. It startled him. As Pinky opened the phone to reveal the text message, he remembered his role as an agent aboard this train. His encounter with Vicky Patterson has momentarily relieved him of his duty to the people aboard this train. *It won't happen again*, thought Pinky, *I won't let my guard down again.* Agent Jordan reached into his breast pocket, but failed to find what he was reaching for. *What the hell? How could this be?* Pinky now frantically patted his pockets to find the object that was suddenly and mysteriously misplaced. "That bitch!" was Pinky's first thought, "she must have took it!" But there was no way of knowing for sure.

One thing was for sure, agent Jordan better find that key quickly before it got into the wrong hands.

***

Vicky Patterson was also washing her face, but in the comfort of her first class washroom. These washrooms were small, but they offered the rich passengers an opportunity to poop in private.

Vicky's face was blushed. Her face was always blushed after a large session of intense love making. Oh how she had missed the feel of a good man on top of her; a man inside of her.

Naturally her husband hadn't been putting out lately. If he we wasn't too drunk to get it up, he was too "tired" to satisfy her. *What a dick.*

Yes, it was a bad marriage. Every time she looked at her husband she seemed to dislike him more. Even now, as she walked out of the bathroom and looked at him passed out on the bed in their compartment, she felt the anger build in her.

But Toby was her priority. Toby was her angel. Toby was her ice cream loving, Nintendo addicted, beautiful child. And Toby would have been devastated if the marriage ended. She just couldn't do that to him.

As if on cue, right then Toby came bouncing into the compartment.

"Hi mommy."

"Hi angel," replied Vicky.

Toby turned his attention to the drunken man before them. "Hi daddy."

"Ughhagfdshsshsg," came the response, muddled, under the breath of the father. His eyes were still closed, but he was half conscious.

"Harvey, would you get up and talk to your child," Vicky pleaded to him.

"ahshsjjssuue."

"Sorry? Could you clarify that," she said angrily.

Suddenly, Harvey shot up in his bed and opened his eyes, directing his accusing glare at Vicky. "I said, shut up bitch," he bellowed.

And that was it. Vicky could not handle this anymore. Her tolerance was at her limit. Her breaking point had finally surfaced.

Right there, Vicky burst into tears. Not just any tears. Tears of hatred. Tears of terror. Tears that suggested a life on the edge of madness. They were tears unlike anything she had ever felt, and certainly tears unlike anything she had ever let Toby witness.

Vicky began to pant and then began to run. She was out of the compartment and into the corridor in an instant. She was finally on her exodus.

Strangely, as she moved about the train, her thoughts drifted to the man she had just been with, the man who called himself Pinky. It was a fitting name. Only minutes before, his pinky finger had been stimulating her clitoris. His pinky finger had been rubbing her sensitive nipples. And ultimately, his pinky finger had been in her mouth, as she had attempted to suck the joy out of his life to interrupt the misery in hers. It was like Pinky and the Brain. He was called Pinky, and she wanted his brain. Any replacement brain would do. Any brain that contained different memories than the horror that she endured on a daily basis.

Where are you Pinky?

She wanted him. She needed him. She would do anything to find him.

Pinky!!!!!

***

Pinky looked at his cell phone. The message that flickered on the screen was going to haunt him for a long time. *Found out? Gone to fix the problem?* These were not good words to be reading right now. "No! Damn it, this can't be happening!" Pinky shouted aloud and slammed his fists against the sink counter. It was time to get involved. It was time he became the CIA agent he claimed to be. *But I need to find that key!*

***

Kevin Hussein was closing in on his target. Not long now until he would be getting rid of this threat. *I know you are on to me... I have to stop you.* Hussein was sweating; his heart beating as the adrenaline soaked into his blood. *The ultimate sacrifice*, the wise words of his predecessor. *The ultimate cost to full-filling a mission.* There was no room for error, no chances left. *This old man has to die, and it has to happen now!*

***

Peter, the white haired old man from the dome car, took out his room key and open the door to his sleeping berth. *Time for a little nap,* he thought to himself. Peter took off his glasses and placed them on the bedside table. He paused, as if contemplating something, then dropped dead as a bullet pierced his skull.

Standing in the doorway was Kevin Hussein, sweat dripping from his dark shadowy figure; a smoking gun ricocheting in his right hand. Hussein paused only momentarily before retreating back the way he came,

- 79 -

carefully closing the door behind him. *Good bye, old man, and my God have mercy on your soul.*

Just outside the old man's sleeping berth, Kevin Hussein turned to see Pinky Jordan standing beside him. "Oh! It's you! You scared the shit out of me," said Kevin Hussein after taking a deep breath of relief. "It is all taken care of, boss. I got rid of the enemy."

"You have done well," said Pinky Jordan. "You have done your duties well." But inside, Pinky Jordan was mortified. *What have you done? Now what do I do? How does this scene make any sense in relation to the plot so far? Am I a good guy or a bad guy? So many questions!*

8

SEXUAL TENSIONS

17:05

Sally was in heaven. It was beyond her comprehension. It was too amazing to fathom. She was having sex with Stephanie Warlock. She was having sex with the girl she had been in love with for the past two years.

Sally's head was currently situated on Stephanie's naughty bits, but it also had a thousand thoughts racing through it at the same time. Her thoughts drifted back to the moment she first saw Stephanie.

Sally had been tagging along with Harry Taves as he escorted her to a hotel near their office building. She didn't really know what they were doing there, but she had her suspicions. Truth be told, Harry was a horny man. He probably had dozens of girls that he met there weekly.

When they had arrived at the room, Harry invited Sally to come in, but she declined. She found it strange that he even wanted her in the room as he got it on with some call girl, but hey, Harry was Harry – a creep.

"No thanks," she had said. "I'll go grab a drink in the bar downstairs. Fetch me when you're finished." *Which will probably be in five minutes* she laughed inside her head.

Sally hadn't noticed the disappointed look on Harry's face as she turned to walk away.

Down in the hotel bar, she took a seat to wait and ordered a drink. When the waitress arrived to deliver it, Sally took a look at her and felt like she was already drunk. She had to be drunk. No woman could be that beautiful without some sort of alcohol to enhance her appearance to others. But no, it was true. Stephanie Warlock was THAT good looking.

"Here's your drink," Stephanie, the waitress, had said. "Enjoy."

Sally replied, "Thanks."

And that was it. That was the only word she had spoken to Stephanie in those two years – "thanks." Sally hadn't been able to muster anything further. She had returned to that bar at least thirty times since then, but she had purposely sat out of Stephanie's section. She was too scared. All she had done was watch. She had sat and watched. She had watched Stephanie from afar. Half the time she stayed and watched so long that she was too drunk to walk by the end of it.

A couple of times, when Stephanie was looking especially luminous, Sally had been forced to retreat to the washroom and masturbate. Her desire had gotten the better of her.

It was two years of love, but it was also two years of torture. In that entire time, Sally had never mustered the courage to talk to her.

Eventually Stephanie had quit as a waitress and taken a job as a bartender on VIA rail. Suddenly those desperate nights of borderline stalking were unaVIAlable to Sally. Unless of course she wanted to pay for tickets to and from Toronto. Clearly she couldn't afford that. Harry may have been horny, but he was as equally cheap.

Sally was expectedly upset but Stephanie's change in setting, but she never lost hope. She always believed in the power of love. She always felt that fate would bring them together eventually.

And now there they were.

Now, Sally had her tongue on Stephanie's lotus patch. Now, Sally was actually giving pleasure to the woman who had always given her so much mental pleasure; pleasure intertwined with torture.

"Harder. Harder!" Stephanie was screaming. Stephanie was in pure ecstasy. Sally was not surprised. She had pictured this moment for so long, she knew that when it finally came she would not be a failure. She had demanded it of herself. *Sally, you must be the perfect lover.*

***

Over the loudspeaker, a female voice interpreted several of the passengers engaged in their... "recreational activates."

"Ladies and Gentleman, *Madams et Mesuires*, your attention please. We would like to welcome everyone to come to the Lounge Car for the VIA rail traditional Disco Party. The party will start in fifteen minutes, *quinze minute see-vous-plait*." The female attendant was announcing the traditional 'VIA rail meet and greet party' that brings all of the passengers together for a good time. I wonder how these passenger's will respond when they meet for the first time...

***

Cassandra brushed herself off and forced a smile. She was servicing drinks down in coach. *Coach,* she thought to herself, *where the drunks hung out.* Cassandra was also thinking about the hobo. *Poor hobo,* she thought softly. She never thought her desires would end up costing someone's life.

After serving drinks to the coach passenger's, Cassandra made her way to the speakerphone to make a public announcement. It was time to announce the train's arrival at its first stop since Winnipeg. It was during this stop that the train would fuel up and take on some more supplies for the next eight hours.

Timson's point was the name of their first stop. The tiny hamlet has home to no more then 100 people, but it did have a radio receiver capable of transmitting signals across the Canadian Shield. For this reason, Cassandra also felt comfort arriving in Timson's Point. *In case anything was going wrong, I could phone it in,* she often thought to herself.

"Passengers, if I could have your attention please. Following the disco, we will be making our first stop at Timson's Point; in about one hour from now. All passenger's wishing to deboard at Timson's Point are asked to grab their on board luggage and head towards the front of the coach car at that time." Cassandra then began to recite the French version of their arrival at Timson's Point. "Bonjour madams et measures. Voul alez arrivez dons lays stationaelle Timson's Point aujeduey. Regardez la sonsationelle bonjour." Cassandra wasn't very good at French, but let's be honest, who is?

Cassandra took a deep breath, sending the memories of her dear hobo to the back of her mind for the time being. *Time to get to work*, she thought to herself.

***

No one was in the luggage car. No one *human*, that is. A barrage of slithering shadows were moving about, making their way towards the door. The door was closed, but they would find a way out. These shadows were very small. They could find their way out of anything.

***

Pinky was drinking. The attractive bartender was currently away, but that could not dissuade him. Minutes ago he had taken a seat at the bar and reached over to swipe a bottle of rum.

Pinky poured himself a double rum and coke and downed it in one gulp. After a murder and losing *the key*, he damn well needed a drink. That disco he had just heard about over the intercom actually sounded tempting. It would be a fine instance to let off some steam.

Pinky was in the midst of pouring himself a second drink when his attention was diverted to the door.

Vicky Patterson immerged into the bar car panting. She was sweaty, out of breath, but still undeniably sexy to Pinky. But that didn't matter. She was just the woman he was looking for. He couldn't believe she had the gull to show herself after stealing his prized possession.

Pinky immediately jumped to his feet and moved to Vicky. He was in her face before she had a chance to react. "What have you done with my key, you whore?"

Through his anger, Pinky was still able to tell that Vicky was upset. Tear streaks were visible on her cheeks. Something was wrong.

Who cares?

"What are you talking about?" Vicky managed to spout out.

"You know damn well what I'm talking about. One minute I'm inside of you, the next minute I've been robbed. Who the hell do you think you are? A damn two-fisted sludge machine? Huh?"

"What! Pinky, you've got it all wrong. I didn't take anything."

"Give it back! My precious key! My precious!" Pinky started to hyperventilate, and had to sit down.

"Pinky…I would never steal anything from you. Please, believe me. I-I-I love you, Pinky. I wouldn't do anything to you to make you upset." Vicky meant what she just said, but until the words came from her mouth she wasn't sure if what she was feeling deep inside was actually love.

"Love?!" Pinky was surprised, "what do you know about love!" His response surprised even him, who found that the rum was probably doing most of the talking at this point, "I mean, Vicky, we just met – how can you be in love with me?"

"But I am, Pinky, I am. I have never met a man that I felt so comfortable with, I man wish such a big... pistol... to protect me." Vicky reached forward to embrace Pinky, but the mood was suddenly interrupted the presence of Stephanie, who was returning for her shift at the bar.

"You!" Shouted Vicky Patterson, as her head turned to see the young bartender pushing through the door. "I know you!"

"Uh-oh," Stephanie knew Vicky Patterson as well.

"You are the bitch who slept with my husband!"

"Husband?" Pinky said, almost to himself, but then a little louder, "you are married! You are a whore! Get away! I can never love someone like you!"

"Listen, lady, I don't know what..." Stephanie was trying to ease the tension, but she wasn't allowed to finish her sentence.

"You do know, you do so now. You better watch you back, missy. You hear? You watch your back." And with that, Vicky Patterson turned to follow her lover down the corridor, but Pinky had already ducked into another car and was out of sight.

The tension left behind in the bar car was almost as thick as pea soup. Love, lust, lost and lonely; four emotions that start with "L" that all landed themselves in the same spot at the same time.

They say some creatures can sense the emotions of other beings. The great Canadian black bear, for instance, was thought to stock its prey based on how depressed it was. The more depressed the prey was, the easier would be for the bear to catch it. Many species of snake were the same. Some scientists believed that snakes were actually attracted to sexual tension, but that theory was left unproven. Until maybe soon?

***

The loudspeaker panged to life, and the female voice from before spoke: "Ladies and gentleman, *madams et mousieurs*, the Disco will start in one minute. All interested are asked to come down to the bar car underneath the front dome car. *Merci bo-coup*."

9

DISCO FEVER

17:37

"Shamus, any word yet from the engineer?" The duty manager was asking the same question every five seconds, it seemed to Shamus.

"No sir, nothing but hisses from the radio interference.

"Shit! How could this be happening!?" The duty manager was about to get another surprise. Just then the door to the control room opened and four uniformed figures entered.

"Are you the duty manager," one asked, as he reached into his pocket to produce a badge. "Inspector Bridges, railway police."

"Oh!" The manager was caught off guard. The railway police didn't usually make an appearance until *after* a train had crashed, something he always resented about the organization. But now here they were in full force, ready to help. "Yes, well hi there, we've got a little situation here, you see..."

"No need to fill us in, we already know what happening. Now I'd like to ask both of you to leave, we'll be taking over matters from here."

"You'll be what..." Shamus was stunned that he was being asked to leave during an emergency like this.

"You heard me, kid. We've got jurisdiction over this mater." It was the voice of another man, this one was not in a police uniform but he did produce a badge. "Special agent Rocko, CIA. Now please, you need to leave now."

"CIA, what the...?" chimed Shamus and his duty manager on cue.

"But this ain't the U.S.of.A. Mister, you can't just barge in here and tell us..."

"I said get *out!*" Rocko was clearly very agitated about something, and it was also very clear that he didn't have time for two railway workers to question his authority.

"Alright, alright!" Shamus got out of his seat and walked towards the door. Come on, man, I can see we aren't welcome here anymore. You guys can take this mess if you want!"

But outside the room, away from the ears of the railway police and CIA agent, Shamus had something very different to say. "Did you hear that last transmission from VIA 01, just as those guys appeared?" Shamus was talking in a very low voice to avoid being overheard.

"No, what are you talking about?" The duty manager wasn't sure where Shamus was going with this.

"I couldn't mistake that sound anywhere," continued Shamus. "That was the sound of a diamond back rattler, no joke." And he wasn't joking; his face was stone cold and dead serious.

"A snake?! Ha!" his manager didn't appreciate what he interpreted as a cruel joke.

"No! I'm serious," Shamus wanted to yell, but he knew he'd better keep his voice down. "Look, man, I'd know that sound anywhere, I grew up on a snake farm not far from here."

"Oh, buck up, boy," the manager retorted. "We've been displaced by the CIA! The fucking CIA! And all you can think about is a stupid memory of your childhood? I'm leaving! Going home! I don't need to get involved in any of this." And with that, the manager turned and walked down and out of the VIA rail control room.

I'm not wrong, Shamus knew. *I need to tell somebody, or else there is going to be pandemonium aboard that train.* Shamus reached into his pocket and dialed the first number that came to mind. *We have to get those snakes off of that train!*

***

Janzo Kim's pilot tapped him on the shoulder, awakening Kim from a pleasant dream involving multiple lady partners. "We'll be in Canada shortly, sir," said the pilot.

"Excellent, inform me when we are about to land. I don't want to miss a single moment!"

"Yes sir," replied the pilot, who turned back towards the cockpit.

I want to be there to see his face when he finds out what I've done! Kim chuckled quietly to himself, then drifted back into his multiple lady partner dreams. *Oh baby!*

***

Toby Patterson was board. His Nintendo was gone, his mommy was in tears about some other guy, and his dad was still sleeping. Not being able to stay cooped up inside his family's sleeping berth, Toby decided to go for a little walk. *I can have fun ALL ON MY OWN!* He thought to himself.

In the corridor, outside his room, Toby saw a faint shimmer coming from a piece of metal lying on the floor. "A coin!" Toby exclaimed aloud, "now I can go buy a soda! Or an ice-cream! Or maybe it's a Toonie and I can buy both a soda *and* an ice cream!" His excitement was met with equal disappointed when he found out that it wasn't a coin lying on the floor, but a key. "Stupid key! What is it even used for, anyways?" The dull, brass key had no insignia on it, nor did it seem to match any of the keys he had seen so far on the train. "Maybe it'll open a secret door some place!" Toby regained some of his previous excitement. *A treasure hunt!*

Toby pocketed the key, and started down the long set of corridors that linked the rail cars together. *I bet I'll find this secret door near the front of the train,* thought Toby. *The baggage car surely has tons of secrets in it!* Young Toby Patterson was right about one thing, there was definitely a big surprise waiting for him at the other end of the train, only this surprise was a lot worse then a soda and ice-cream.

***

Passengers started to assemble in the bar car. The mood was cheery: music flowed from the speaker system while Stephanie Warlock prepared drinks. At first, only a few people mingled, but soon, after a couple drinks, the atmosphere turned joVIAl and many men and women could be heard talking and laughing, while others started dancing and letting loose. The voyage from Winnipeg to Toronto, after all, was 36 hours long – a long time to be sharing a little tin railway car with a hundred other people. And so, for the last forty years, the VIA employees continued the tradition of a disco 'meet and greet'.

"Wow, good music!" A tall, slender man wearing a cowboy hat and plaid jacket said to a young woman standing beside him. "The name's Jed, I'm from Texas, and let me tell y'all a little strange up here in Canada, but I've grown to love it. You Canadian women have got some kinda 'yahoo' about you that is a real turn on, and I mean real!" The man winked at the woman.

"You want to make out?" The woman said, impressed by the man's exotic accent.

"Yeeehaw! Save a train ride a cowboy! Come on darl'n!" And the two started making out right there in front of everyone.

"Boy, I wish I could do *that*," an older woman in the corner said, tilting her head towards the young couple.

"Well why don't you try?" A gentlemen who had heard the conversation from the bar stepped over and offered his hand.

"Goodness me!" The woman let out a laugh as she embraced the man with her red lips.

"Some party, eh?" Stephanie turned to see Jack standing neatly beside the bar counter.

"Oh! Hi Jack, haven't seen you for a while!" Stephanie was eyeing Jack's fresh attire and clean smell.

"I was doing some thinking, Steph," said Jack, as he took a sip of his rum and coke. But Stephanie wasn't listening, she was eying the way Jack's pants fit him so well.

Oh, to be married to a gay man! What a treat that must be.

"Steph, I really like you, and..." Jack was interrupted by Stephanie, who suddenly seemed to realize where this conversation was going.

"Meet me in the bathroom in five minutes, okay hun?"

"Oh! Okay then!" Jack was stunned. His friend had told him how this type of cologne would attract girls. "I saw it on a commercial," he remembered is friend saying. " You just spray it on, and all these girls come out of nowhere wearing nothing and have sex with you!" *Nice advice, indeed!* Jack cooed to himself. *Stephanie Warlock will be mine!*

Across from the bar, Sally had arrived at the disco just in time to see Jack talking to Stephanie. She then watched as Stephanie left the room, Jack in tow. *Noooo! This can't be!* But it was true, the love of Sally's life was about to sleep with another person... a man! A gay man! Sally's blood started to boil, a wave to regret washing over her. She scanned the room and saw an older man standing near the window, a beer in his hand. Without thinking, she grabbed the man and started sloppily making out with him. The man, who seemed to be quite drunk already, gladly accepted the favor.

Emotion levels inside the bar car were getting hotter and hotter by the second. The emotions, undetectable to humans, slowly started drifting back through the train where some very different animals were starting to take notice. The sexual tension aboard VIA rail 01 would soon prove disastrous.

10

SHOWTIME

18:00

Toby Patterson peered through the window in the door that led to the baggage car. *Where are all of the grownups?* He wondered. In fact, all of the adults were hitting up the disco, including the staff. Toby took a deep breath, then pushed the door open slightly. A wave of warm, nauseating air flowed out from the baggage car, forcing Toby to put his hand over his mouth.

"Hello?" He called out. No response. "Hello, anybody in here?" He squinted to see through the dim light, and didn't see or hear anyone. He opened the door fully and entered.

Look at all this stuff! Toby was glad he found somewhere cool to explore. Inside the dark, musty room, Toby felt his way to a large pile of personal luggage. "One of these keys has to work here!" Toby said aloud. He fumbled in his pocket and took out the brass key he had found not long ago on the floor of the train. He examined the choices before him: suitcases, duffle bags, boxes and... what was that there? A metal box with brass latches and a slot for a key. "This must be your home, key!" Toby bravely placed the key into the box and turned it. A dull *thud* sounded the release of the locking mechanism. Toby then undid the latches. He didn't know why, but something felt really uneasy, as if someone, or something, was watching him. The latches undone, Toby was able to now open the box. Inside was a green canister and a warning label: "Danger – may result in injury, death, or teen pregnancy. Keep out of reach of children."

That's it? Thought Toby. It looked like a fancy bottle of Mr. Clean. He took off the lid to the bottle and smelt it. *Phew!* It melt awful. Not wanting to linger too long, Toby put the lid back on and walked out of the baggage car with the canister. Careful to hide it from view, Toby darted back through the train to his berth. *That was enough adventure for one day*, he thought. *Maybe I'll take a nap or read some comic books...*

The eight year old boy had no idea what he had just uncovered. He also had no idea that the door to the baggage car was still open after he left.

***

Back in Winnipeg, Shamus McGunty had found a pay phone and was now frantically talking to an old family friend, Dr. Cutchinson.

"Are you sure, Shamus," the voice of Dr. Cutchinson said through the phone's receiver.

"No doubt in my mind!" Shamus was talking to the one person who he knew would believe him. "There are snakes on the train."

"Dear God," the old doctor sighed, "you need to tell the police!" Dr. Cutchinson had experienced wild snakes before. He remembered flying back from Hawaii on a 747 when a bin of snakes stowed below the passenger cabin suddenly exploded open, killing several of the passengers as well as both the pilot and co-pilot.

"But the police aren't listening to me!" Shamus had tried to tell the police, but they simply laughed at him. *Ya right, kid, snakes on a train. That sounds like quite the story!*

"Ok, ok! We need to act fast, then. Any ideas?"

Shamus had an idea. It was risky, but it could work.

"Jeeze-us! That is too risky son, count me out!" The old doctor said after hearing Shamus's plan. He didn't want to get involved at his age with something so dangerous.

"Fine, then I'm going myself. Someone has to go and save those people! Dr. Cutchinson, I suggest you contact all of the snake wranglers in the county as well as get an anti-venom supply put together. I'll contact you as soon as I can!" Shamus hung up the phone, and then dialed another number. He hoped that he still had a few connections down at the railway station in Toronto.

***

Pinky was not at the disco. *How could that woman sleep with him when she was married to someone else!* The memory of his time with Vicky in the janitorial closet brought a tear to his eye. She was some kind of woman, though. *And my key, how could I have lost the key.* Pinky collapsed his head into his hands.

"You okay," the voice of Kevin Hussein interrupted his sorrow.

"Ya, yes I'm fine," said Pinky softly.

"Good, because it's almost time to begin our mission. We'll be arriving at Timson's point in fifteen minutes. I need you to be strong now, Roger."

Pinky still wasn't used to being called Roger. *A stupid made up name*, was how he reacted when Rocko first gave him the assignment. But it was true, he needed to be strong right now if he was going to be successful in completing his mission. He couldn't worry about some woman now, there were far too many things to worry about of much greater importance. "I'm good to go, Hussein."

"Okay, Roger, let's get down to the baggage car and unleash the fury!" Kevin Hussein was a bloodthirsty killer, and it was obvious that the thought of killing all of these people aboard the train excited him.

"Let's lock and load," said Pinky, as he repositioned his pistol in its holster. *Showtime*.

***

It just so happened that at that exact same moment, 30,000 feet in the air, Janzo Kim was also getting ready for something big. His pilot had informed him they were about to begin the decent into Sudbury, Ontario. "Showtime," said Kim to himself as he buckled his seatbelt and got ready for the descent.

11

FIRST STRIKE

18:05

Everyone was dancing. Dancing and making out. The disco was a huge success, and random hook-ups had completely overtaken the car. Not just the car, the whole train.

Above the passengers, a large disco ball twirled, creating a lush and romantic atmosphere. The music was very seventies, but everyone seemed to enjoy it. The people felt so alive. Their legs could not stop moving to the beat, and their tongues could not stay out of each other's mouths. It wasn't just a G spot, it was a G bloc party. It was beautiful.

Maybe too beautiful.

Everyone was so preoccupied with horny thoughts and the rhythm of their bodies that none of them had any chance of noticing as a sea of slithering figures slowly made their away into the car and onto the dance floor, discreetly moving about the people's dancing feet.

At first, the attack was slow. As the random screams gave way to desperation, however, the impetus for a complete breakdown of social order started to transform the passenger's aboard VIA rail 01 into a mob; a frantic, desperate mob. The snakes, as if summoned by an invisible force, began their merciless attack on its human inhabitants.

Two minutes ago, the mood in the bar car was almost orgasmic. Singles and couples alike were dancing, flirting and making out. The orgy of human inhibition spreading like wildfire; as if the emotions in the room were an airborne virus traveling from host to host, infecting each person with waves of pheromones. Two minutes ago everything was well and good.

The snakes, capable of sensing human pheromones in very small concentrations were going mad over the pheromone concentration levels in the bar car. It was enough to send into mating mode – which also happens to make them extremely dangerous and extremely unpredictable. They may attack without any notice or instigation.

At first, only one snake attacked. Instantly, passengers nearest the door where the snake slithered through started to yell and scream. Not knowing what was happening, passengers only the other side of the railcar started to head towards the screaming. The snake, sensing the dangers around him, instantly attacked its first victim, the young woman who, only moments ago, was making out with the Texan named Jed.

"Oh shit! Oh shit! I've been bitten, help me, help me!" But the passengers didn't want to help, they wanted to run. Everyone turned to run at once, leaving some people trapped at the end of the line. A second snake then appeared from the door and lurched towards an older man, biting him on the throat. Almost instantly, the poison from the snakebite entered the man's blood stream, making his blood boil. His face and neck started to swell from the strain of the toxins in his bloodstream, cutting off his air supply. He would die a few seconds later.

"Oh my God! Run, run!" random shouts from the passengers only escalated the violent behavior of the snakes. A third snake appeared, a giant green rattlesnake. The snake's tail shook, the tell tail warming of an attack. Snap! The snake chomped at the balls of another passenger, sending him bleeding and screaming in random circles.

"Ahhh! Fuck you snake! Quit chomping my nuts!" The attack continued. Several more snakes appeared. Some were orange and red, others green and brown. All of them had huge fangs.

Cassandra was trying to climb on top of the bar counter, the slight elevation providing her with some temporary protection. She grabbed a bottle of Jack Daniels and threw it down onto a snake that was trying to coil up the barstool. The bottle shattered, and sent the snake flying back. Several pieces of glass pierced his scaly skin, but the snake was not dead. He was only more pissed off.

"Why won't you die you stupid snake!" Cassandra reached for another bottle off the shelf. But the bottle she was blindly grabbing for was not a bottle, it was a snake! A smaller cobra was now starring straight into Cassandra's eyes. Cassandra starred back, in momentary disbelief. Then the snake attacked. It went straight for Cassandra's arm. The shock of the bite made Cassandra violently recoil her arm. The snake flew off and landed back on the floor. Blood and puss dripped from the two deep incisions in her arm – pain shot up a moment later, followed by an alarming sensation. Her arm was going numb. Her brain was racing. *I have to get the poison out of my hand*! In a frantic maneuver, Cassandra took a beer bottle from the counter, smashed it open then used the glass shards to cut her own arm off. A wave of nausea overpowered her as shock from the trauma of loosing her arm from a beer bottle made her pass out.

Nearby, a much larger snake was taking its time sucking the life from an elderly woman who had fallen dead from a bite. The bowa-constrictor preferred to eat its prey slowly and in one giant gulp. A human being would take days to digest.

The mob was slowly exiting the bar car to the adjacent diner car. Once in the diner car, they should be able to close the door and keep the snakes out. Unfortunately, some people were not going to make it in time. The snakes were approaching fast.

Two more bites and Vicky's drunken husband and another woman fell dead. Sally was standing next to the drunken man and woman who got bit. She was pushing the person in front of her when all of a sudden she lost her footing and fell down. When she tried to get up, people who were in line behind her stepped on her back. "Ahhhh!" she screamed. "Get off of me, get off of me!" But the mob wasn't listening. It was every man and woman for himself or herself. Sally was finally able to get off the ground and push herself to her knees. That's when she noticed the giant green snake starring back down at her. Sally only had a split second to avoid the snake, as it lurched towards her lotus-patch. *The pheromones! Hissssss! Hisssssssssss!*

Sally recoiled and made a run for the safety of the door that led to the diner car. The snake turned in pursuit. Sally made it to the doorway, but in enough time. The snake had caught up, the sneaky bastard! And in another attempt to kill, it lurched skyward towards Sally's G-spot. BAM! The snake hit its mark and bit hard. "Ahhhhhhhhhhhhhhh!" the blood curdling cry of Sally could be heard from the end of the train.

***

Did you hear that? Stephanie Warlock paused. Jack Baytel, who was on top of her, stopped too. Together they listened. Screaming! *The passengers were screaming!* "We have to go", said Steph as she raced to pull her pants back up.

"Its probably nothing!" said Jack who really wanted to finish what he started.

"No, I know that sound. That is Sally. She is in trouble and I need to help her!" Stephanie did up her uniform and rushed from the janitorial closet in which she and Jack had spent the past ten minutes. *The sex wasn't that good anyways*, mused Stephanie, who now realized that Sally was her one true love aboard this train. *I'm coming Sally, I'm coming!*

***

Sally grabbed the snake with both hand and yanked it from her lotus-patch. The bite wasn't that bad, but some poison definitely got in to her. If she didn't get that poison out quickly, she would surely die.

"Help! Help! Oh God, please help!" She pleaded. Then, an answer came as if from the heavens. *The voice of an angel.*

"Sally! Sally, oh god what happened, don't worry my love I am here for you! I won't ever leave again!" Stephanie Warlock grasped Sally's hand and pulled her to safety in the diner car. The door closed tightly after them, trapping the snakes in the first four rail cars. "Oh no! Sally, what happened?"

"They bit my...you know, down *there*," even on her deathbed Sally was still a modest person.

"Looks like she has suffered from a snatch attack," said some random passenger.

"I'm not going to let you die. You hear me! I won't leave you! You can't leave me. Now, together we are going to make things better!" A tear flowed down Stephanie's check as a wave of guilt flooded her heart. If she hadn't gone to have sex with Jack, she would have been here sooner. *It is all my fault!*

"Dear god, that woman is going to die unless we can get help right away!" Voices of some of the passengers broke the stillness of the diner car.

"What can we do?" Stephanie begged. "We don't have any antivenom on board!"

"Someone is going to have to suck the poison out!" Another passenger stated. "That is the only way she'll live!"

Stephanie knew what to do. "Can I get a little privacy, please!" Some of the passengers turned away, while others got in for a closer look.

"S-s-teph, getting... w....weak...please h....hurry!" Sally was going more and more pale by the second.

"Hold on, sugar," said Stephanie reassuringly, as she bent down and began to suck.

12

STRANDED

18:45

All of the surviving passengers were gathered in the dining car, terrified. All of them had something different on their mind.

Vicky was panicking about Toby. She hadn't seen him since she had run out of their compartment in tears, and now she had no idea where he was. Hopefully he was still there. All she knew is that her husband was dead.

Harry Taves was glad to be alive, but even more glad that he was about to be even richer.

Cassandra couldn't stop thinking about how much it sucked that she had lost her arm. But hey, it was better than being dead. She had just fastened a belt around her joint to stop the bleeding, but it certainly stung to lose an arm.

Jack was still overwhelmed by the fact that he had just had sex...with a girl.

Pinky was filled with remorse. This wasn't supposed to happen. The snakes were not supposed to have gotten out this early. And now dozens of people were dead. The plan was to release them immediately before getting off the train at the first stop. Of course, it was Pinky's mission to ultimately prevent that. Now he had failed. Those people were dead because of him.

Sally wasn't really thinking. She was beyond thinking. It is hard to think when you are in immense pain at the same time as having a massive orgasm. Pain vs. bliss, and because of Stephanie's great sucking ability, bliss was somehow winning.

Stephanie was thinking about her love for Sally as she sucked and sucked. She was also thinking about the bad taste in her mouth.

And then there was Kevin Hussein.

Kevin looked down at the display before him. A woman was performing fellacio on another woman right in front of him. Normally this would be occasion for celebration, but Kevin was beaming with horror. *What are we going to do now?* Pretty soon the train would be making its first stop. Everyone would vacate the train, and no more deaths would take place. He had failed. His mission had failed. The snakes had done their intended job. They had attacked relentlessly; they had attack without mercy, all because of the great amounts of sexual tension in the air. But they had done it prematurely. How had they gotten out?

Stephanie pulled back from Sally. She was finally out of breath. She had a mouth full of poison, and it was causing her to gag a bit. She rose to her feet and spat out the window.

"So, she spits," remarked Jack. Too bad he didn't get to find that out for himself.

Sally was still in agony, but already people could see that she was feeling better. Her breathing was now steadier, and her moaning was a bit happier sounding.

"Stephanie, you saved me," she said.

"You would have done the same for me."

I already did Sally slyly thought to herself.

Stephanie took Sally's hand in hers and pulled her to her feet. The whole car of people looked at them in amazement; looked at them with great affection. They had all just witnessed true love at work. There they all were, in a situation of pure terror, with their lives in grave danger, and yet they all couldn't help but feel a bit nostalgic for the love before them. On top of that, everyone still felt extremely horny.

After a pause, Cassandra finally spoke up, "So what do we do now?"

Chattering erupted from the crowd, the fear starting to surface in their voices once again.

"It will be ok," Pinky announced. "Our first stop is in just a few minutes. The snakes won't get to us before that. We're home free."

"But why hasn't the engineer stopped the train already?" interjected Vicky. "I mean, people are dead."

Pinky just shook his head. "Are you insane? We're in the middle of the Canadian wilderness. We couldn't possibly stop here."

"Yeah," Kevin continued. "If we got off here we'd be in even greater danger than we already are."

"I hear that those beavers are smelly and deadly," added another random woman.

Regardless, everyone seemed to calm a little bit at the prospect of stopping. Safety was within their grasp.

***

Casey Mactavish lay lifeless. A snake was slithering out of his mouth. He was as dead as a doornail.

And the train waged on.

***

In the dining car, the passengers glared out the window. They saw lights approaching them from out of the distance. Timson's Point! They were almost there.

The excitement was overtaking all of them. Soft cheering started to grow softly within the crowd. As they got closer and closer, the cheering grew louder.

"We're almost there," Cassandra was shouting, as she pointed towards the lights with her one remaining hand.

Pinky, however, felt that something was dangerously off. No one else seemed to notice, but the train was still moving at top speed. As a trained CIA operative, he knew that trains typically begin to slow a few miles before reaching a destination. But now here they were, so close to their destination, and the train had not slowed in the least. If anything, it was going faster.

Eventually those same worries began to enter into the minds of the other passengers. The excited faces started turning to looks of concern. The train was now fully immersed with the surrounding light of various buildings. They were in the town. They were in Timson's Point, but the train continued to shoot forward.

"What's going on?" interjected Vicky.

"Something is wrong," Pinky half replied, half said to himself.

Panic once again erupted from the crowd. Everyone was at the side of the car, looking out at the town as it shot by them. "No!" was everyone's shared response.

Eventually a train platform came into sight. Dozens of people stood there, awaiting the arrival of

VIA rail 01, but their faces stared bewildered as the train refused to stop.

This could not be happening. Everyone was so desperate to get off the train. They could not take this.

Harry Taves spoke up, "I can't believe this." And he wasn't having it. Taves grabbed a nearby chair from a dining table and hurled it at the window. The impact made a slight crack in the glass, but nothing substantial.

"I'm getting off this train," he continued. Taves picked up the chair one more time and started to violently smash the glass, over and over. More splinters began to form on the glass.

Several other passengers seemed to like his idea. Before long there was four or five men smashing chairs into the glass in a desperate attempt for escape.

"What are you guys doing?" Pinky inquired. "We're moving way too fast. You can't get off."

"Well I'm not staying here," shot back Taves. He took out the tiny safety hammer above the window marked "Emergency Exit" and gingerly tapped the four corners of the window pane.

SHATTER!

His efforts had succeeded. The entire pain of glass came splashing to the floor in a heap of shards. The intense sound of a steaming engine flooded the room and wind began to pour in.

Taves made a move for the large opening and got ready to jump.

"No! Pinky grabbed at Taves by his suit jacket and began pulling him back. "You'll kill your self you ignorant fuck!"

More people came to Pinky's aid, holding Harry back from certain doom. Surprisingly, he gave little resistance. Subconsciously he seemed to be just as aware as the others that it was a stupid plan.

"Look," Sally shouted, pointing. Everyone veered outside once again to see the lights fading away. The train was now fully past the Timson's Point train station and was quickly moving out of the entire town.

"It's too late anyway," said Pinky. "We can't leave. We're almost back into the dangerous Canadian wilderness."

Gasps came from the crowd.

"Never mind these fucking snakes. We leave and we'll have even bigger problems on our hands; like a giant moose or something."

"Hey, how about the emergency stop!" an excited young woman piped up the obvious solution to there problems.

"No...."the one armed Cassandra Funk gasped over the pain to respond, "...we can't use the emergency stop. Some....*gasp*....teenagers a while back started pulling the stop for fun...... we had to..... *gasp*..... disconnect them all!"

"Those fucking teenages," shouted Taves, "always ruining things for us. First its $1.00 beers, now its emergency stops. Fuck!" Harry Taves was near the breaking point. His exasperation was shared by the rest of the stranded passengers.

"Clearly something has happened to Casey," Cassandra fought to declare.

"Who the fuck is Casey?"

"The...the train's driver." Cassandra began to worry for her old pal. "Someone is going to have to....*gasp*....go to the locomotive and manually stop the train....I could do it....but....I don't have the arm needed to activate those brake levers.... it will have to be someone strong!" Cassandra Funk was gasping for life as she scanned the crowd for a volunteer who could save them all from certain snake death. But that volunteer faced an incredible challenge: go to the locomotive, past the snakes, to activate the brakes manually. At first, it seemed that nobody was going to volunteer, but then a confident voice broke the silence.

"I'll do it!" Jack Baytel stood forward, eyes hardened in determination, fists clenched in retribution. He had just had sex, and with it came the strength he needed to save these people. "Now, Cassandra, you'll have to tell me how to activate those brakes when I get there...."

13

LONE HERO

19:15

Jack was ready to go.

The plan, as they had decided, was simple – Jack would get up on top of the train and move to the engine car. Cassandra didn't quite know what would be the best way for him to get into it, but Jack felt that he would be able to figure it out once he got there.

At the back of the dining car, the crowd gathered to see him on his way.

"Good luck," muttered several of the survivors.

"Thanks. I've already had some pretty good luck today, so this she be a piece of cake," Jack replied, with a discreet wink towards Stephanie. In the back of his mind, he couldn't help but think that this was the best way for him to prove himself to her. *That Sally girl had got nothing on me.* After all, he was possibly about to face a hundred poisonous snakes. Sally, on the other hand, had only managed to get herself bit on the crotch.

"Here, take this," said Pinky, handing Jack a single butter knife he had found on one of the tables. "You might need it."

Jack nodded his thanks and then turned and opened the door leading to the gangway between the dining car and a sleeper carriage. Outside he began his descent up the ladder.

It wasn't long before he was pulling himself onto the dining car's roof. He found it surprisingly easy to stand once he was up there. *It's not like in Mission Impossible* he thought. But that was just a movie. This was real. Jack had to keep reminding himself of that.

Jack moved swiftly to the other side of the dining car. He used the moon's bright glow to guide his way. Despite the horrible ordeal they were all in, it was actually a pretty nice evening.

Beside Jack, kilometer upon kilometer of Canadian forest whizzed by silhouetted against the moonlight. If Jack fell off the train, not only would everyone aboard surely die, but if he survived the fall he would be right in the middle of some of the most ferocious forests in the world. The consistent sound of the locomotive humming and the metal railcars jigging against the rails, however, muffled what was probably extremely eerie sounds coming from the dense foliage.

Gaining strength and momentum, Jack was approaching the glass dome portion of the railcar. Using the glass as a cover against the wind, Jack peeled off his shoes and socks – the bare feet offering more grip and stability then his Birkenstocks. Then, positioning himself on his belly, he used his hands and knees to slowly maneuver himself over the dome. *Just like Spiderman*, Jack thought to himself.

After passing across the dome car, Jack had another challenge: the jump from the dome car to the coach car. Although the gap between the railcars wasn't the large, the chance that he wind would propel him backwards into the crevasse was a real possibility. *This ones for you, Steph*, thought Jack, as he reconciled all of his strength for his leap of faith. He took a final, deep breath and sprinted towards the gap.

The jump was a success, however Jack lost his footing slightly as he landed onto the top of the coach car roof. "Shit!" He exclaimed, as he clambered to stay on balance. Using the rills upon the top of the train car, he was able to slowly regain his poise. *That was close*, he thought to himself. *Too close*.

Traversing the coach car was easy compared to the dome car. Soon, Jack was ready to attempt another jump. This time, he needed to clear the coach car and land on the baggage car. The wind seemed to blow even stronger now, as if the gods had it in for poor Jack. Taking his time to make sure his footing was how it needed to be, Jack took a second deep breath and a second leap of faith.

BAM!

The weight of Jack's body colliding with the steel roof of the baggage car sent shockwave through the inside of the train. Below him, several hundred snakes slithered away if violent procession.

I've almost got you now, thought Jack as he regrouped and forged on towards the locomotive. One last jump left – the one that connects the baggage car to the train's locomotive. Already, Jack was becoming aware of the heavy exhaust being produced by the engine's diesel motors. *One last jump, and I'll be in the locomotive.* His mission was almost a success.

Jack once again poised himself for another jump. This time, Jack had a feeling for the air resistance and horizontal motion – this jump should be easy. Jack relaxed slightly, having gained more confidence. This would prove to be a deadly mistake.

Jack jumped. But he didn't land properly. He landed sideways, the wind quickly pulling him towards the side of the locomotive. Jack began to slide off the train. Below him, the steel rails and gravel beddings flew past at a seemingly blinding rate. "Ahhhhh!" Jack was going to die if he didn't act now. Then , as if some force of God was taking control of Jack's reflexes, the butter knife entrusted upon him came from his pocket and dug into the siding of the railcar. The knife now provided Jack with enough stability to pull himself up and regain control. *The butter knife.*

Sweat dripping porously from his skin, Jack stood up on the edge of the locomotive that he had jumped to and gazed back towards the direction he had come. *Wow.*

Then, as if karma had somehow caught up with Jack, the giant entrance to a tunnel carved into a granite cliff appeared in the darkness. Not noticing its sudden appearance, Jack was instantly decapitated by a protruding rock face.

SKE-DUSH!

Jack was dead. His mission was unsuccessful, and the train continued to barrel on without a driver.

***

Fifty miles down the same set of railway tracks, another emergency was about to start.

A hundred car freight train, carrying petroleum products and dynamite, was thundering down the rails a full speed. The engineer on board was casually monitoring the train's systems when suddenly the radio sparked a warning. Not expecting a radio transmission for a further five miles, the engineer jolted upright and, in the process, knocked his coffee cup over, spilling its contents over the control panel of his locomotive.

"Oh Shit!" the engineer cried out as sparks shrouded his instrument display.

"CN freight 672, this is control, come in 672," sounded the dispatch controller in Winnipeg.

"This 'ear is freight 672, what can I do you for?" the engineer said, trying to hide the fact that he had just spilt boiling hot coffee all over the place.

"672, we have an emergency. VIA rail 01 is out of control. Stop immediately and pull of onto siding 146 – five miles ahead."

"Roger!" The engineer immediately heeded the warning by instinctively reaching for his brakes. When he pulled the lever to slow the enormous freight train, however, the breaks didn't even budge.

"What the hell?" The engineer muttered. *The coffee has fried the breaks!* He tried again, still no response from the breaking units.

"Umm…control this is 672," the engineer said sheepishly.

"Go ahead 672," replied the dispatcher.

"We've got a problem over here. My breaks, they are totally fried! I can't stop this thing!"

"You're fucking serious?" The dispatcher said, obviously annoyed.

"I'm getting the hell off of this time bomb!" And with that the engineer opened his driver side window and jumped from the speeding locomotive.

14

SHAMELESS SHAMUS

19:21

Shamus McGunty was feeling a little air sick. He hated to fly, but he especially hated to fly in helicopters. Beside him, a mustached, sunglass wearing pilot was frowning at Shamus's Idea.

"You are some reckless fool, my man." The pilot could be heard saying through the headset Shamus was wearing. He continued, "I mean, I have to give you some credit for wanting to help these people... but a runaway train full of snakes... well that's just ludicrous, dude."

Shamus eyed the middle-aged pilot, then responded, "if I don't help them, who will?"

The pilot, who didn't really seem to care if *anyone* actually did save these 'train folk', as he had derogatorily said back in Winnipeg. "Well, jeez I don't know!" He finally said, exasperated that he was actually flying his helicopter overtop the rail lines, pushing the throttle hard to catch up with the speeding passenger train.

"Hey!" Shamus suddenly shouted, "look! The train, I can see it!" And sure enough, the distant outline of a train could be seen in the distance on the tracks below.

"Well I'll be," the pilot said frankly, "we actually caught up to it." The pilot was skeptical that they would even make it to this step in the plan. "I'd say we are still about half an hour out. You better get yourself ready, dude."

"Roger," Shamus said. He then took off his headset and turned towards the back of the helicopter, where a pile of gear and boxes was stacked messily. *What the hell am I doing?* He thought to himself, as he began to prepare himself for his shameless act of courage.

***

Not far away, at that very same instant, Janzo Kim was landing in Sudbury, Ontario. His 747 touched down and started to brake hard, the airstrip not being ideally suited for a plane this large. Moments ago, the control tower had cleared them for landing, but when the controller looked up now to see the size of the approaching aircraft, he freaked out.

"Airwave 72-9er, what the hell do you think your doing! You can't land here, your way too big!" Kim's pilots ignored the warning and landed anyways. Between Kim's pilots, they had logged well over 7000 hours of flight time in the 747. The exotic places Kim liked to travel to often meant landing at smaller airfield.

"72-9er, you are a lucky son-of-a-bithc!" The controller exclaimed over the radio. He was commenting on how the 747 seemed to come to a stop only metres from the runway threshold. "72-9er, you are clear for taxi to parking Delta, via taxi ways Tango Victor Foxtrot."

"Tango Victor Foxtrot for airwave 72-9er," the pilot responded. He was also relieved they were safely on the ground. *Fucking Janzo Kim*, he often thought during these crazy voyages, *always wanting to travel to such desolate places.*

The truth was that Kim liked to be present when he was trying to kill someone. He had seen enough action movies to know that if you wanted a job done right, you better do it yourself. Not that he didn't trust his two operatives on board VIA rail 01. He simply liked to be there incase he was needed.

A limo was waiting on the tarmac for Janzo Kim. Kim wasted no time deboarding the plane. From the airport, the limo would drive them to Sudbury

Junction, the railway station on the other side of the town. There, he would wait to hear from his operatives aboard the train who by this point in time should be safe and sound at Timson's Point. If he didn't hear from them, he would know that something went wrong. So far, he hadn't heard from them, but this was not a surprise – radios didn't work very well in this part of the world. But he was getting anxious.

***

"A lot of time has gone by." Stephanie was just stating what everyone else was thinking. It had been almost half an hour since Jack had left on his voyage, and there had been absolutely no word from him since.

Stephanie was naturally pretty worried. She had just had wild sex with Jack, her homosexual buddy, but it wasn't her sexual affection for him that had her worried. Stephanie had decided that Sally was in fact the girl for her. She didn't suck venom out of the lotus-patch of just anyone. *It must be true love.*

But Jack and her shared another type of bond. Out of all of the horny businessmen she dealt with on a daily basis, he was the only one she felt actually understood her. He understood how desperate she was. He understood that it was not her first choice to pour drinks to shallow entrepreneurs. She was doing it for her daughter. She was doing it because she had to.

And now look where it had gotten her - trapped on a speeding train with hundred of deadly snakes roaming around. *God life sucks.*

"What are we going to do?" Cassandra asked. "We can't wait around forever."

"Yeah," Taves spoke up. "Those snakes will find a way in here."

Oh how right Harry Taves was.

***

Inside the bar car, the snakes had been doing some planning of their own. As they all slithered around, searching for a way of getting to their human pray, one snake with an orange trim had made its way up the wall and into an air-conditioner duct.

The other snakes liked the idea.

Soon every snake in the car was following suit, making their way through the duct; a duct that happened to lead into the adjacent car.

***

Vicky was now alone. Unbeknownst to the rest of the group, she had snuck out of the dining car and towards the back of the train. She was on a mission to find her child.

Toby was somewhere, and she had to find him. She just prayed to God that he wasn't in any of the snake occupied cars. For all she knew, he could already be dead. But she couldn't believe that. She wouldn't believe it.

"Toby. Toby!" she called out, always to no avail.

Vicky was now in one of the sleeping carriages, desperately searching every bed. Her ultimate destination was their own compartment. Toby knew better than to spend too much time walking on his own, so the best bet was that he had returned there.

Eventually Vicky made her way into the car with their compartment. She made a quick search of a couple of the rooms before hers, and then came up to the door of theirs. "Toby?" There was no response.

Vicky opened the door. She walked in. Her eyes went wide when she saw what her son was doing.

***

Pinky Jordan saw an opportunity to leave the group for some much needed secret agent alone time. The truth was agent Jordan just noticed that his cell phone had two bars of reception, and he needed to make a call.

In the privacy of the observation car, the last car in the train, Pinky dialed a number. A ring confirmed the call had made a proper connection.

"Rocko here, go ahead," the reply on the other end of the phone became audible in Pinky's ear.

"Rocko. It's Jordan. Where are we at?"

"The mission is going well," replied Rocko, "we have the control room – the employees here know nothing," Rocko said.

"Good. But we have a problem aboard the train, sir," Pinky now had to confess to Rocko the mission aboard the train wasn't going as planned.

"I know, we heard over the radio, the snakes are out already, aren't they?" Pinky was surprised the Rocko already knew.

"How..." Pinky started to respond, but was interrupted.

"The train is out of control, Jordan, and I'm afraid I have some more bad news for."

Of course, Pinky thought, *they would be able to see the out of control train from Winnipeg.*

"There is a freight train up ahead on the tracks, Jordan. We have to act fast, otherwise the entire train will crash."

"Fuck!" Pinky shouted aloud. "How long do we have?"

"About one hour, agent Jordan. You know what has to be done before that hour is over."

"Of course."

"We're counting on you."

"That's what scares me." At that, Pinky ended the communication and began to make his way back towards the dining car.

***

"Toby, what do you think you are doing?" Vicky raised her voice to her son.

Nestled on the bed, Toby lay before her with his "thing" out and his hand wrapped around it. Toby was masturbating like there was no tomorrow.

"M...mom...what are you doing here?"

"Are you kidding me, Toby? People are dying on this train and you're doing that. Is this your attempt to gratify the situation?"

Toby didn't really know what his mom meant, but he could tell she was deadly serious. He quickly zipped up his pants and stood up.

"What do you mean people are dying?" he asked him mom, an ounce of fear invading his young mind.

"I mean hundreds of poisonous snakes are on this train, and they're killing people. And now I walk in here to find you handling another snake."

Out of the corner of Vicky's eye, she couldn't help but notice a random canister sitting open on a nearby table. However, she didn't think much of it. She was still too in shock from what she had just discovered.

"Anyway, come on, we need to get out of here," Vicky said, reaching her hand out to her son.
Toby took her hand and together they turned and existed the compartment.

Vicky led Toby through the corridor, back towards the others. They were just about to exit the sleeping car, when out of nowhere they both collided with another figure as it exited a compartment. Vicky made a slight shriek and was knocked back slightly, but Toby actually fell to the ground.

It took them a second to compose themselves before they were able to identify who had run into them.

Pinky!

"Jesus Christ," was Pinky's response.

"What are you doing here?" Vicky asked.

"I was about to ask you the same thing," Pinky responded as he knelt down to help Toby to his feet. "Are you ok there sport?"

"Yeah, I think so. But this ain't helping my blue balls," replied Toby.

Once again, Vicky gasped in horror. "Where did you learn that expression young man?"

"I dunno, video games."

Pinky had to smirk to himself. This one was interesting family he had gotten hooked up with.

"Alright, we need to get back. Let's go," Pinky announced. Now he was leading the way, as the three of them started back towards the dining car.

***

Hussein was sitting alone in the dome car with his headphones on. While everyone else was partying at the disco, he was taking some time to listen to some music and rest up before he needed to get off the train. But according to his watch, the train should have stopped ten minutes ago. And oddly enough, everyone aboard the train seemed to have vanished. He took off his headphones for a second and found that all the noise from the disco below him had mysteriously ceased Hussein decided he better take a look around. He got up and descended the steep staircase that partitioned the dome portion of the railcar from the bar.

At the bottom of the stars, Hussein turned to see if anyone was at the bar. But there wasn't. Everything was eerily silent. Then, out of the corner of his eye, he saw the outline of an arm sticking out from behind the bar.

"Looks like everyone had a *little* too much to drink," Hussein mused to himself. He breathed a sigh of relief. *I'm not going crazy after all*, he thought.

Hussein went over to the bar to see who it was. *Maybe it's a lovely lady passed out over there*, he thought to himself. Hussein leaned over to see who belonged to the arm, but the answer would send cold shivers down his spine. The arm was detached! Something, or someone, had ripped it off its body!

"Of shit!" Hussein turned to flee, but found himself starring face to face with a giant orange snake, who was recoiled, poised to strike.

15

WHAT'S FOR DINNER?

19:45

Cassandra was sitting at a table, clutching her arm. The pain had not subsided since she had been forced to remove her own arm. It wasn't like your typical cut, where it started to feel better over time. No, losing an arm was a whole new ball game. Who knew?

Stephanie came up to Cassandra with a glass of water. "Here Cassie, drink this. It will help with your nausea."

"Thanks." Cassandra painfully took the glass and sipped at it. *Oh this is so horrible.*

All the other surviving passengers had settled down a little bit. Most of them had taken seats in the dining car, just trying to catch their breath. The snakes had shown no sign of having gotten out of the adjacent bar car, so somehow they had all managed to relax a bit.

That didn't mean the fear has subsided.

At that time, many of them couldn't help but think about home, to think about their loved ones. Would they ever see them again? It was an emotional time for all of them. Aside from the fact that they had all just witnessed a dozen people lose their lives; they were also all being forced to face their own mortality.

At that point, it seemed unlikely that Jack was coming back. The train was not stopping. It hadn't even slowed down. It was hard for them admit what that probably meant, but they were forced to.

Stephanie especially was struggling with the reality. *Jack,* her sweet pal Jack. The man who had just penetrated her had also just been sent to his own death. Literally, one hour she was riding him, the next hour he was dead. She was certainly happy that she had been able to save Sally, but she also cared deeply for Jack. He was just such a nice man, even if he hadn't made her achieve orgasm.

It also probably meant that Casey was dead. For all they knew, everyone was dead; everyone except the fourteen passengers that remained in the dining car.

"Ladies and gentleman, I have an announcement," it was the voice of Pinky Jordan as he re-entered the dining car with Vicky and Toby. The entire car went silent to hear what he had to say.

"Now, don't panic people, but we are on a collision coarse with a freight train." His words were short and to the point. It took the passangers a few moments to realize the importance of what he was saying.

"W-w-what?" Sally stuttered over her words as reality swept over her. They were all going to die. "What can we do?" she managed to ask the question everyone had on their mind.

"What the fuck?" Harry Taves, who was pretty quiet up until this point – which was pretty uncharacteristic of him. "How do you know this?" Taves was obviously skeptical of Pinky's revelation.

"I-I-I can't tell you that..." Pinky hadn't thought that the passengers would question him.

"Then why the fuck should we fucking believe you, you asshole? Who the fuck do you think you are?"

"This is agent Jordan of the CIA, ladies and gentlemen, and I love him!" The voice of Vicky Patterson rose above the crowd. Her words descended upon them like a warm blanket.

"You with the CIA," said Jed, the Texan man with the cowboy hat. "Boy howdy! The calvary is here! we are saved!"

"The CIA?" Taves seemed to be very started by that comment. "Oh-oh shit! You are here to..." But he was interrupted suddenly as the door to the diner car opened. Kevin Hussein staggered through, gasping his neck. Two small punctures gushed blood onto the floor.

"Roger.... Roger.... I..... failed! I failed....Roger....I.....sorry...." Hussein was out of breath. He collapsed on the floor of the diner car. "Roger...I....snakes.....out.....early....I...."

"Who is this man? Do you know him, Pinky?" Vicky, like the other passengers were startled by the appearance of the dark stranger in the dining car. "Why is he calling you Roger?"

"I-I don't know, I think he is crazy. Let's just ignore him," Pinky tried to diffuse the situation. *A wrong move at this point would cost him the mission.*

"....Roger.....Pinky?....what......the......fuc.... k" Kevin Hussein dropped to the ground, his hand dropping from his neck. A giant snake bit was revealed to everyone.

"He's been bitten too!" Yelled Sally.

Kevin Hussein died on the floor of the diner car. But his dying words lived on.

"What was he saying?" Demanded Harry Taves, "who the fuck are you?" His demands were echoed by others.

"Pinky? What was that man saying... he was lying, right?" Vicky Patterson starred into the eyes of her lover. "Are...are you not from the CIA?"

Pinky was about to explain everything – how he was sent here under cover on a very secret mission – but he remembered his oath. He couldn't break his promise the homeland.

"Don't worry, people, we are going to get off this train! Everything is going to be all right," Pinky said.

"Well, I am. Don't be so sure about yourself," was the reply from Harry Taves.

Boom!

Pinky found a fist in his face, as Taves decked him. Suddenly the two of them found themselves in a tussle, as Taves continued to pound at Pinky, who was simply tying to defend himself.

"Stop it!" pleaded Stephanie.

But it was no use. The two of them went at it and at it until they found themselves rolling on the ground.

Eventually Taves found himself with the upper hand. He was on top of Pinky as he pulled back for a finishing blow.

And then Pinky pulled his gun.

Taves stopped dead. He lowered his punching hand, frightened off by the sudden appearance of a gun in his face.

The entire car went into hushed silence. No one knew what to think.

"Get off me, mother fucker," Pinky said calmly.

Taves did as he was told. Pinky was able to get to his feet, as Taves backed away, the gun still pointed at him.

"Stop it!" Cassandra suddenly exploded. "Stop it stop it stop it!"

Everyone in the dining car looked to the one armed stewardess, as she stood from her chair. No one said a thing.

"This is ridiculous," she continued. "Why the fuck are we fighting with each other when we clearly have other problems on our hands?"

Cassandra now had everyone's full attention. No body said a word as she loudly and desperately spilled out her emotions. There she stood, weeping, clutching her severed arm, her uniform covered in blood. She had officially had enough.

"Look at me for fuck's sake. I lost my fucking arm. The car next to us is filled with dead bodies, and there is a shit load of snakes on this train just itching to get another chance at making us their dinner. So please forgive me if I find it fucking ridiculous that someone just got a gun pulled on them.

"Taves, you're an asshole, just so you know. And Pinky, whoever you are, I don't exactly trust you. But we need to get along. You need to stop fucking fighting. So far today I have snapped a hobo's spine as he rocked my world with his massive pole of power, I've had a snake gnaw into my arm, and I've cut off my own arm to prevent the poison from spreading. And now, here we all sit, the lone survivors, and we're fighting…and we're horny. We're all still so fucking horny. I'm still fucking horny. I don't understand why, but I'm horny, and all I want is to be penetrated by the first thing I see. Somebody explain that. But we can't. You can't explain it. Why? Because we don't have time. We don't have time for any of that because we still need to get ourselves out of this bloody mess. So we're going to stop fighting and we're going to start working together, understand. The first thing we're going to do is…"

HISS!

Without warning, a snake landed on Cassandra's other arm. It seemed to fall out of nowhere as her speech was suddenly cut short.

"Aaaaaahhhh," Cassandra screamed. The entire car of people erupted into panic once again.

The snake began biting into Cassandra's good arm. Blood splattered against the wall and she frantically flailed from side to side, trying to get the snake off of her.

"Cassie," Stephanie screamed, and she rushed to her aid. Cassandra was all over the place. She would not stand still. The other passengers had to move out of her way as she smashed against the walls, the windows, the tables, doing anything to free herself. But the snake would not let go.

The snake chomped and chomped. Cassandra continued to scream, until finally the snake was off of her.

But so was her other arm.

The snake had bitten clean through it, and now Cassandra was left with no arms. She looked to the floor to see the snake slither away, leaving her severed arm lying in a puddle of blood.

"Noooooo," she screamed.

Stephanie managed to grab at Cassandra (what was left of her) and pull her out of harms way. Everyone looked up just in time to see an entire legion of snakes suddenly drop into the dining car out of a vent above their heads.

"Everyone get down," yelled Pinky. He took out his gun and fired several well aimed shots at the snakes. Four snakes dropped dead, several more were wounded.

"Mommy! Get me out of here!" the young voice of Toby Patterson could be heard screaming above the gun fire.

"Everyone, let's get out of this car, follow me!" It was the voice of Vicky Patterson. Seeing her son frightened half to death evoked confidence in her. "To the sleeper cars!"

The sleeper cars awaited behind the diner car. Another door would separate the passengers from the snakes. *But how did the snakes get in to the diner car?*

Vicky looked up and saw a snake drop from an air conditioning vent. "They are coming from the vents! Quickly, we needed to stop them!"

Pinky understood. He turned and fired a couple of rounds into the air-conditioning duct, sending it crashing to the ground. The snakes that were housed inside it also came crashing down. The passengers ran as quickly as they could. Sally grabbed Cassandra, who was too week to run by herself, and helped her towards the door. Pinky fired the last shot from his magnum then turned his attention to Vicky and Toby. They were like family to him now, and he had to protect them.

Not everyone was able to make it to safety. The attacking snakes had dinner with several more passengers. In the skirmish, the snakes had bitten an older couple on the neck, the Texan man on his chest, and a young woman on her ass. They all succumbed to their wounds in seconds. These snakes contained a very aggressive poison.

Harry Taves almost got bit himself, but managed to use his briefcase to smack one of the snakes aside: "Take that, bitch!"

The remaining passengers made it the door of the sleeper car. Only ten passengers remained, including Pinky, Vicky, Toby, Sally, Steph, Cassandra and Taves. The door to the diner car was shut, once again trapping the snakes from reaching them.

"Now what do we do?" said Steph, who was helping Sally care for Cassandra.

"Now we fucking sue VIA rail!" yelled Taves.

"We have to stop this train! We can't stay here anymore," yelled another passenger.

"That's right," said Pinky, recalling that the train was on a collision course with a freight train. "We have to get off this train soon, otherwise we're all gonners."

***

Janzo Kim was now at the train station in Sudbury. Soon, the VIA train would enter the station and he would make sure that the snakes had done their job. He would make sure Harry Taves was dead.

Kim looked at his watch. One minute until the train was due at the station. Soon, the faint rumbling of a train could be heard. *Why hadn't he heard from his agents yet?* Kim was sweating slightly as he glanced at his watch again. *Something was wrong! Damn it!* Kim clutched his gun, which was carefully hidden inside his jacket pocket.

The low rumbling of the diesel locomotive grew louder and louder.

Kim knew that there was a chance plan A hadn't worked. It was an admittedly wacky plan, but Kim had always prided himself on his creativity. To him, killing wasn't just killing - it was his art.

Regardless, sometimes art bombed. That was why he bothered to arrive in Sudbury. Plan B involved Kim killing Taves himself.

The rumbling train suddenly came into view. But it was going way too fast. Kim watched as the speeding locomotive rushed past the station. It didn't even slow down!

"We have a problem here!" yelled Kim to his assistants in the company limo. "I need to get to that train! I need to see if anyone is alive on board"

16

DEADLY SEX

20:02

The horror was over for the surviving passengers on board VIA rail 01...for now. They had opted to move past the first sleeper car and into the next one, attempting to put as much distance between them and the snakes as they could.

Already several people were busy blocking the overhead vents in hopes of preventing a repeat of the close call they had all just narrowly escaped. Pinky was stuffing some carry one bags into the vent to cut off any possible passageway for the snakes, while Vicky had found a roll of tape in a compartment and was now using it to cover up all the axis points.

Still, everyone was feeling somewhat strange.

Cassandra couldn't describe the way she was feeling. There were two glorious girls taking care of her wounds. One was a long time co-worker, Stephanie Warlock. Another was an attractive business woman named Sally Knight. And for some reason, above all the pain, Cassandra wanted to do them both – right here right now.

Strangely enough, Pinky Jordan was feeling the same way about Vicky Patterson. The woman with whom he had had sex with earlier was breathing heavily, as the adrenaline rushed through her body and made her flush.

And for another strange reason, Harry Taves was suddenly and inexplicably attracted to his sandwich.

In fact, everyone aboard the train was starting to feel extremely horny. As Cassandra has mentioned, they were always feeling that way, but as soon as they entered the sleeper car it started to come one extra strong.

"Did the snake bite you anywhere else?" Asked Sally, as she examined the state of Cassandra's flesh wounds.

"Well....now that you mention it....I think one of the snakes bit my breast. If I had a hand, I'd check. But I don't."

"Let me see," cooed Stephanie, who was feeling extremely horny. "Oh! My goodness, you have a bite on your breast, look Sally!"

Sally looked over, but didn't see any bite mark.

"Oh no! Is it okay?" asked Cassandra, obviously concerned.

"I don't know, what do you think, Sally?" said Steph, as she passed a wink over to Sally.

"Oh! well, I think we'd better get her into bed and look after that poor breast, do you conquer, Steph?"

"I conquer, Sally." Sally and Steph helped Cassandra up and led her towards an empty sleeping berth. *So hot!*

Vicky has just put a final strip of tape on a vent opening when she found Pinky standing right next to her. He was just staring at her, his eyes emitting an elegant glow. For a bunch of people who had all just escaped death, they were all acting rather strange. But Vicky didn't care to think about it. All she could think about was Pinky. She returned his gaze, and together, they got lost in each other's eyes.

"You doing ok?" Pinky finally asked.

"I think so," she responded. "I've been better."

"Well maybe I can help a little bit." With that, Pinky took Vicky into his arms and kissed her passionately. They kissed for what seemed like an eternity. Vicky wouldn't have cared if it actually had been for eternity.

Eventually they parted lips and looked at each other once again. "My compartment is just over here," Vicky said alluringly.

"Is it now?" Pinky replied in a confident tone.

Together they turned and entered Vicky's compartment.

Left behind, Taves was gazing hard at his sandwich, even stroking it a little.

As for Toby, he found a nearby washroom and went to relieve a bit of tension.

***

Shamus opened the door to the helicopter. The strong wind whistled into the cabin, momentarily stunning him. *It was time.* Shamus was wearing a black harness; a steel cable connected him to the helicopter.

Up ahead, on the railroad tracks, the familiar sheen of the VIA train's metal passenger cars reflected the faintly lit sky. The sun was now set, and only a faint twilight remained on the horizon.

The mission was simple, yet extremely dangerous. Shamus had to repel from the helicopter on the roof of the moving train. From there, he would make his way to the locomotive and stop the train. Then, he would save the passengers. *And try not to die in between.*

Shamus looked down at the two large, black bags also attached to his harness. Inside the first bag were various anti-venoms he was able to collect from Dr. Cutchinson. Inside the second bag was something Shamus hoped he wouldn't have to use – a high-powered semi-automatic machine gun, loaded with amour tipped bullets. *Just in case*, he told himself. But Shamus knew all too well that a train full of snakes wasn't something you take lightly.

"You ready back there?" The pilot turned to Shamus, obvious anxiety floated in his voice.

"Ready as I'll ever be," replied Shamus in a confident voice.

Shamus had grown up on the snake farm, and he learned quickly the need to be tough. When he was six, his older brother had pushed him down a steep hill near their house. After tumbling down and down, Shamus found himself face to face with a black bear. Stricken with panic, Shamus tried to run but found that his legs weren't working. The black bear, which happen to be protecting her young cubs, reared back on her hind legs and let out a warning growl. Shamus tried again to get up, but this time realized that his left leg was actually broken – he was a sitting duck. The bear heeded another warning, and then charged towards Shamus. Then, as if everything was happening in slow motion, Shamus suddenly found his inner strength. He knew then what he had to do to survive. Grabbing a stone that lay beside him, Shamus managed to hit the bear right in the eye. The bear recoiled, letting out a cry of pain. She then snarled and charged again. But this time Shamus was ready. Using his good leg, he managed to jump onto the bear's head. Then, using his swiss army knife, Shamus sliced the bear's throat. The bear gasped for air – red foamy blood spattering over the dense, leafy forest floor. Shamus struck again, this time piercing the bear's eyes.

"Fuck you, bear!" the six year old Shamus cried. It was the first and last time he would ever swear.

The bear stood, momentarily stunned, then fell dead.   The young bear cubs, now left motherless, appeared from their hiding. Shamus, realizing what he had just done, picked up one of the cubs and carried it home. He raised that bear all on his own. He named it Charlie, and he cared for it like it was his own son. Then one day Charlie got too large, and when Shamus came home from school he found Charlie – dead on the barn floor – shot between the eyes by a high powered rifle. His father, believing that the bear was getting too dangerous, had shot him. Shamus never forgave his father for that. He vowed, from that day on, to use the power of the mighty bear to save lives, rather then destroy them.

"Shamus....yo! Shamus... you there, buddy?" The pilot's voice awoke Shamus from his boyhood memory.

"Oh! Yes, sorry, I was just reminiscing," Shamus said, blushing slightly.

"Well we're right overtop the train now," said the pilot. And indeed they were.

And now we wait for the arrival of our hero from above. Will he make it alive? Will the passengers survive their ordeal? Stay tuned and find out!

***

Pinky was zipping up his fly. *That was a doozy* he thought to himself.

Vicky was lying naked in bed, the sheets up over her body. For the second time that night, she had just made sweet love to Pinky Jordan. But this time was different. This time seemed almost weird. After all, they were all in a life or death situation, yet for some reason they had found time to get it on. Frankly, hot sex should have been the last thing on their minds.

"That was great," Pinky remarked, but he himself was also just feeling the utter strangeness of the situation. It was almost as if...

And then he saw it.

Pinky had been so caught up in his horniness, he hadn't even noticed the open canister sitting on the table.

"Where did you get that?" he asked.

"What?"

"That," Pinky repeated, gesturing towards the canister.

"I have no idea," Vicky replied. "I've never seen it before."

Pinky couldn't believe this. There it was, the canister. And opened.

"Oh God," he muttered. "This is really bad. Really really bad."

"I don't understand," Vicky said. "What is that thing?"

Pinky was mesmerized by the canister. His thoughts were racing, and his eyes would not turn away from it. Everything was making sense to him, but it also wasn't. He felt extreme lust for this woman, but he also felt something more. Suddenly all the thoughts he was feeling were put into question. Did he truly have feelings for Vicky, or was it all manufactured?

One thing was certain – he didn't want it to be manufactured.

"That," Pinky finally replied, "is the key to our undoing."

***

Something was in the air as the snakes battled, aggressively, attempting to gain access to the first sleeping car. The dining car, which they currently occupied, was now littered with bodies. But it wasn't enough. The snakes wanted more. Something was attracting them. Something was telling them that they needed more blood; that they needed to continue their pursuit for human victims.

The humans couldn't hold them off forever. They would get there, and soon another train car would be filled with bodies. Soon another car would be filled with DEATH!

17

JANZO KIM

Janzo Kim was pacing back and forth impatiently. Fifteen minutes had gone by since the out of control passenger train flew past him at Sudbury Junction. He now needed a way of getting on board the train. If Harry Taves survived, not only would his business fall to his bastard son, the deadly secret Taves held would be leaked to the world.

It all happened two years ago. *Its like it was yesterday*, Kim always thought to himself. Harry Taves was actually employed by Janzo Kim in Kim's downtown office in Shanghai. Taves, a straight-talking North American businessman, stood out from the rest of Kim's employees, and not only because he is white and they are all Asian. No, it was because Taves was good at his job. He was better then good – he was ruthless.

Harry Taves could make a business deal any time, any place, under any circumstances. And with

Taves as his right hand man, Kim was quickly soaring to the top of the trinket market universe.

Kim was initially fond of Taves – his blunt attitude about work was a sign of true loyalty in Kim's eyes. Kim even invited Taves over for Thanksgiving diner when Taves had no family to go home to. But it wasn't long until there relationship changed for the bitter worst.

On one cold, rainy day in the countries downtown capital, Kim came into the office to pick up a briefcase he had forgotten the day before. It was a Saturday, and all of the employees were gone for the weekend. The building was quiet *almost too quiet*, he remembered thinking. Kim entered the elevator and punched the number "31", the top floor of the office tower. When the doors opened, Kim was shell-shocked to see Harry Taves, behind Kim's own desk, clutching a brown envelope in his chubby right hand.

"Taves...what the fuck....?" Kim didn't have time to finish his sentence. Harry Taves was too quick to respond.

"Looks like we meet for the first time for the last time," said Taves, as he slowly eased himself from behind the desk.

"You! You are the one! You are then one who has been stealing from me?" Kim was almost crying. He had entrusted everything to this man and now here he was, double crossing him.

"Yes, you idiot! It was me! *Can't believe it took you so long to figure that out!*" Taves let out a deep belly laugh, and then reached into the brown envelope he was clutching.

"Don't you dare!" replied Kim, seeing what Taves was about to do.

"Oh yes, my friend. Don't think I won't do it!" Kim shouted back, as he pulled out a pile of white papers from the envelope.

"But why, Taves. Tell me why?" Kim couldn't believe this was happening. *Maybe I'm just dreaming.*

"Karma," Taves said flatly, and then "you had this coming for a long time, my Asian friend!"

"You won't get out of here alive with those. I have guards downstairs. You'll never get past them!"

"You under-estimate me, Kim." Taves reached into his pocket and produced a small revolver. "Now! Up against the wall!" He waved the gun towards Kim, beckoning him against the far wall, away from the elevators.

"You won't shoot me, I know you better then that," but Kim wasn't sure who this man was anymore. The Harry Taves he knew for two years was now a completely different person.

"Don't fuck with me, asshole. You've been fucking your daughter now for five years. I now have all the proof I need to put you away for good. You sick bastard, you even kept the photographs," Taves kept his gun trained at Kim's head as he coolly looked down at the pornographic photographs.

"You asshole! You wouldn't dare tell anyone! I'd be ruined!" Kim was desperate, "how much! How much would I have to pay you! Anything!"

"I want you out of business!" Taves asserted.

"W-w-what? Are you fucking out of your mind! Out of business!"

"You heard me"

"Never!"

"Then prepare to be exposed!" Taves turned towards the emergency exit. Unbeknownst to Kim, he had a helicopter waiting for him outside on the roof.

"I'd rather die." And with that, Janzo Kim leapt towards Taves.

A gunshot rang out. But it sailed just wide of Kim's head. Kim landed squarely on Taves, knocking the gun cleanly from his hand. But that wasn't enough to stop Taves, who was about to put his biggest competitor out of business for good.

"Take this!" Taves exclaimed, as he managed to take out his can of bear spray and jettison its contents into Kim's eyes.

"Ahhhh! My eyes!!! I'm blind!!! Noooo!" Janzo Kim backed off of Taves, his hands covering his stinging eyes.

Taves wasted no time. He got up, exited onto the roof from the fire escape and got into the waiting helicopter.

Taves had escaped that day, remember Kim, standing beside the track in Sudbury, *but he won't escape me today*.

"Sir!" yelled one of Kim's assistant, who was standing beside the limo on a cell phone, "we have a ride! We'll be mobile in five minutes."

"Excellent. I can't wait to see the look on that man's face when I pull up."

***

Stephanie was putting on her bra. She felt the sensitivity of her nipples burn as the spandex overwhelmed her body. Sally has just done a number on her chest, and it showed.

Sally, meanwhile, was pulling up her pants. *That's a lot of sex* she thought in regards to the evening she had just endured. First she had lived her ultimate fantasy - finding herself caught in between the legs of her one true love; then she had that same girl perform a sort of sucking surgery on her genital region; and finally, another spontaneous episode in a sleeping car. Truly, there was a God.

Nevertheless, it was all strange. It seemed weird to experience three sexual episodes in a night when you're also fighting for survival. But Sally refused to complain about the sex.

She would, however, complain if she lost her life on that night. Sally, despite the persecution she had endured for her lifestyle, was a very religious person. At that moment, she could almost picture herself going before the pearly gates, frantically complaining about her "time." *How could God take me at the very time that I discovered true happiness?*
If he did, her faith in humanity would be indefinitely strained. Things had just turned around for Sally, but of course, karma was a bitch. Now she was facing a legion of snakes; snakes that were desperately seeking her flesh. It wasn't fair, to say the least.

"We should probably get back," Stephanie said, interrupting her thoughts.

"Yeah," Sally replied.

Stephanie opened the door, and together they stepped out into the corridor. No one was there. The train almost seemed like a ghost train. Stephanie could almost swear she heard crickets. Then again, it could have been a hissing sound. Given their current predicament, that seemed far more likely.

"Where is everybody?" Sally questioned.

As if on cue, suddenly everyone appeared. Vicky and Pinky came stumbling out of another compartment, while Toby exited the bathroom. The only people still missing were Harry Taves and Cassandra. Interesting.

"Mom!" Toby proclaimed. He made his way to Vicky's side. She put an arm around him.

"And what were you doing young man?" she asked nonchalantly.

"Just some personal therapy," he replied.

He really is a sharp kid Pinky thought to himself. Pinky was almost admitting to himself that he liked the boy. He liked him like a father. It was very strange.

Pinky, Vicky, Toby, Stephanie, and Sally all converged in the middle of the car. Despite the terror, they all seemed undeniably happy.

"Where are Taves and Cassandra?" Pinky asked abruptly.

"I don't know," a few of them responded together.

Just then, the lot of them heard a rustling. It was coming from a compartment right beside them. Their attention all veered to the door. Deep down, it seemed wrong to investigate further, but their curiosity got the better of them.

Stephanie approached the door in question, with everyone else close behind her. She reached for the knob and slowly eased the door open. What they witnessed was a truly disturbing, albeit beautiful sight…

Harry Taves was sitting on the floor, his pants around his ankles. Cassandra, armless and full of agony, was straddling him, riding his man-sword as if it took quarters.

But Harry did not have his hands on Cassandra. Instead, they were occupied by a game controller. As Cassandra satisfied herself, Harry did the same, peering over her shoulder at a TV screen and indulging in a game of Mortal Kombat. It almost beared the likeness of a threesome – Harry, Cassandra, and Sub-Zero, all locked together in a frenzy of enjoyment.

Wow, he really does like his video games Toby thought as he witnessed the debacle.

"Ahem," Stephanie muttered under her breath.

Harry stopped dead with his fingers. Cassandra halted her writhing. They both looked to the doorway.

"Oh, hello," Cassandra said. "We were just...uh...."

The five people in the doorway exchanged glances. Vicky even tried covering her son's eyes, but it was no use. This was a sigh worth seeing.

"Sorry to interrupt," Stephanie finally spoke up, "but we should probably return our focus on the issue at hand."

"Yeah," Pinky continued. "And I have something I need to tell everyone. If we could all meet in Vicky's compartment in five minutes, I need to let you all in on a little secret."

Taves and Cassandra looked at each other, their "parts" still connected. This was certainly a bit awkward.

"We'll be right out," Cassandra said.

And with that, Stephanie closed the door.

***

"Excellent, its perfect!" Janzo Kim was like a boy in a candy shop. In front of him was a parked railway inspection vehicle – a half ton pick-up truck with a set of collapsible steel rims capable of allowing the truck to drive on the railway tracks. The truck idled loudly, its powerful diesel engine ready and waiting.

"Sir, shall I drive?" One of Kim's assistants starting walking towards the driver's door.

"No fucking way! Move over!" Janzo Kim opened the driver's door to the truck and climbed in. Kim put the truck into first gear and positioned it on top of the railroad tracks. He then pulled a lever and lowered the steel rims to the rails. "Welcome aboard the death express – next stop, complete annihilation!"

18

COPTERS AND CANISTERS

Although it was a rather pleasant summer evening, the air rushing by Shamus McGunty as he repelled from the helicopter was freezing cold. Shamus was awkwardly shimmying down from the copter, the bright search light from the helicopter's fuselage illuminating a small target circle on the metal passenger car below. Shamus was on the radio with the pilot, who was controlling his decent.

"Keep it coming, little more…. Little more!" Shamus shouted into his headset. In the cockpit, the pilot struggled to keep the controls straight and level. Outside, the black silhouettes of the Canadian boreal forest was flying by at a dizzying pace.

"Almost…a little more…." Shamus was almost touching the metal railway car with his foot, when suddenly the copter veered violently to the right.

"Damn!" The pilot was fighting a sudden cross wind from a gap in the forest the suddenly appeared.

The copter almost clipped a tree before the pilot was able to gain altitude and reposition the helicopter over the train. Starting again, he slowly started to lower his lone passenger down towards the speeding train.

"Ok, this time we have it.... A little lower....a touch left.... Almost...almost.... Got it!" Shamus' foot touched down first. A metal clang echoed above the howling wind.

"Cut it loose!" The pilot shouted, who was eager to disconnect and head back to base.

"Shoot! It's stuck! I can't get it undone!" Shamus was trying to disconnect the carabineer that was clipping him to the steel cable.

"Quickly! Disconnect it, disconnect it!" The tension in the pilot's voice rose above the static of the radio.

"Damn! I can't get it, it's really stuck!" Shamus was using all of his strength, but the lever on the carabineer wouldn't budge.

"Cut the rope! Cut the rope!" The pilot screamed into the microphone. Up ahead the tracks doglegged to the left.... *If he didn't disconnect before then...*

Shamus was struggling to get his knife out. "Almost have it!" But the wind was making it difficult.

"Oh God!" The pilot managed to say, as the tracks slowly started to bend left. The pilot started to turn along with the tracks, but the pilot knew that he might not make it. Below him, Shamus McGunty managed to get his knife out. He was starting to cut away at the cable.

"Almost got it!" Shamus was still communicating to his pilot. Up above him, the pilot was managing to hold his line with the turn. In the darkness, it was impossible to tell if he was going to be able to pull it off.

"Got it!" Shamus yelled into the microphone as the knife finally broke through the cable holding him to the copter. "Go! Go! Go!"

Up above, the pilot let out a long sigh of relief. *I've done it, I'm the best pilot in the world.* But his victory was short lived. Out of the darkness came the dark mouth of a tunnel. Both Shamus and the pilot saw it at the same time. Shamus immediately hit the deck and narrowly missed death as he was plunged into darkness.

The pilot, however, wasn't as lucky. Instantly, the chopper exploded into *nothingness* as it plowed into the tunnel entrance. Shamus McGunty was left helplessly starring back at the receding explosion as he lay on the speeding train – the echoing sounds of the diesel locomotive in the narrow tunnel slowly becoming the only sound left in his ears.

***

The seven surviving passenger onboard the snake infested train heard a BOOM. It came from outside, somewhere nearby.

"What was that?" Sally inquired.

"It sounded like an explosion," offered Stephanie.

"Nah, it was just an animal," said Harry Taves. "They are vicious in these parts."

Everyone had gathered into a single sleeping carriage. Cassandra, still woozy from her lack of arms, was nestled in between Stephanie and Sally on the bench, while Pinky, Vicky, and Toby sat together on the bed. Harry Taves chose to stand, leaning against a wall.

Pinky had been the one to gather them, and the other six sat with equal amounts of curiosity and apprehension. They were, after all, still in a dangerous situation. They were still under attack from the snakes, and they were still careening towards another train.

"So what's this all about?" Stephanie directed towards Pinky.

Pinky didn't answer right away. He seemed pensive, as if trying to find the right words to say. Finally, after a long pause he produced a single canister from behind him. He held it up for all to see.

"What is that?" Stephanie asked.

"It's complicated," Pinky responded.

"So uncomplicate it."

"Has anyone here been feeling, well, a bit strange tonight?" asked Pinky.

"You mean aside from the fact that we're all terrified of the hundreds of snakes desperately trying to kill us," Sally responded cynically.

"Besides that," Pinky continued. "Have you noticed any strange behavior, in both you and everyone else?"

Nobody responded. They all looked at him questioningly. What did he mean?

"Did nobody find it kind of strange that we all just took a break from trying to save ourselves to, how shall I say, ease some tension?"

Nobody had really thought about it. But now that he mentioned it, they had to admit that it was somewhat questionable behavior.

Pinky continued. "The truth is, this train has been a fucking brothel tonight. Everyone is screwing everyone, and nobody seems to have even the slightest reservations about it. The VIA might as well be for Viagra."

Vicky managed a smirk. *He's so clever.*

"This canister is the reason for that," Pinky finally explained. "It contains a chemical known as afrohotinessliaphane. It activates horniness people. It has been around for centuries and was first discovered by the Knights Templar in the twelfth century and has been hidden in Christian scripture ever since."

"The Knights Templar?"

"Yes. It was their belief that afrohotinessliaphane was the true cause of Mary losing her virginity, thus conceiving Jesus Christ while under its spell."

"You mean that this afro..whatever, created Jesus," asked Sally.

"No, I mean that both Mary and Joseph were under its influence when they...got it on."

"But that doesn't make any sense," said Stephanie. "Mary *thought* she was a virgin."

"Yes, she did. That's because afrohotinessliaphane also contains a no-recall agent. Anyone who suffers under it had no recollection of any of its effects, or what transpired while under them. And I am sorry to tell you all, but tonight, we have all come under its affects. It is the reason for our extreme horniness."

"So Mary wasn't a virgin?" Stephanie continued with her questions,

"No, she was fucked, and she was fucked hard. She just didn't remember it," Pinky explained.

Everyone could not believe this. It was unbelievable. It was truly beyond belief. Anyone who believed this would be unbelievable.

But it was true. They could see it in Pinky's eyes.

"Are you saying that we're not going to remember our encounters; that we're not going to remember any of this?" asked Sally, rather desperately.

"That's exactly what I'm saying," Pinky replied.

Pinky stood from his sitting position and walked to the window. Through the glass he could see the vast Canadian wilderness rush by. He quickly opened the window. "And staring now," he began, "we have exactly half an hour before the effects wear off."

With that, Pinky chucked the canister out the window. The afrohotinessliaphane being emitted into the air had stopped. Their extreme horniness was coming to an end.

***

Shamus opened his eyes. It was dark. The wind was howling. It was cold.

Slowly regaining his thoughts and emotions, Shamus was starting to realize the fullness of his situation. He was now on top of the speeding VIA passenger train. His mission was to save the people aboard from a fuck load of snakes.

After taking a deep breath, Shamus was able to role over onto his belly and start crawling forward, towards the locomotive. *If I can get to the locomotive*, he thought to himself, *I can stop the train and advert disaster!* Shamus was able to get up onto his knees, then his feet. Soon he was comfortably standing – his strength returning to his him. *The pilot is dead*, he concluded, *I am now alone*. But the truth was that hundreds of slithering beasts occupied the railcar on which he stood. He was not alone.

Shamus soon recovered his strength. He started to walk forward, against the wind, towards the front of the train. A stone look of retribution and remorse covered was on his face. *I've had enough of these mother fucking snakes on this mother fucking train!*

***

Back in Winnipeg, Rocko was yelling into the microphone. "You are going to crash, VIA rail 01! Stop! For the love of god stop! You are only 10 miles from crashing into the freight train!"

But nobody was listening.

***

"I'm confused," said Cassandra. She was not the only one. "How did you know about this...afro...hot...is...somethingthane again?"

"Ya, wait a minute, why the shit are you so smart all of a sudden," Harry Taves demanded.

"Yes, tell us please!" seconded Stephanie and Sally in unison.

"He's a CIA agent!" shouted Vicky as she remembered her first encounter with Pinky in the conductor's closet. *Standard issue CIA*, Pinky had said. Vicky was so disappointed that Pinky's manhood bulge was actually a gun, that she had forgot all about *why* Pinky had a gun in the first place.

"A CIA agent!" exclaimed Stephanie. "We are saved! Oh Pinky, our savior!" The other passengers also cheered, but not Harry Taves. Taves went stone white, as if he had just seen a ghost.

"Taves?" probed Sally, "you okay, boss?"

"W-w-what...are...you doing here?" Taves managed to stutter. Pinky turned towards Taves, his blue eyes cutting deep into the conscious of Harry Taves.

"You know why I'm here, Taves...." but the stern voice of agent Pinky Jordan was suddenly drowned out by a high pitched scream of terror. Everyone turned to see a massive python wrapping its body around Cassandra's neck. Cassandra, who now had no arms to protect herself with, was watching helplessly as the snake slowly positioned itself for its final strike.

"Run!" screamed Vicky, who grabbed her son's hand and headed for the door. Everyone else followed suit, including Harry Taves who seemed all to glad for the interruption.

"Cassandra, no!" screamed Sally, but there was nothing Sally could do. The massive snake was now fully in position. The snake paused slightly, as if toying with its helpless prey. Then, after a quick flick of its forked tongue, it lurched towards Cassandra's neck. But it never found its mark.

All of a sudden the entire train seemed to lurch violently backwards. Everything and everyone inside the railway car flew forward, including Cassandra and her slithering assassin.

"Ahhhh!" screamed all of the passengers as they were helplessly tossed aside like cows in a tornado. Toby was thrown from his mothers grasp and collided with the door frame head first. He let out a small cry then fell into unconsciousness.

Stephanie fell directly on top of Sally, their voluptuous bodies colliding together with tremendous force and hotness.

Then, as quickly as the ordeal had started, it ended with a violent screech and a thud as the entire train slammed to a complete halt.

Pinky was the first to say something. "We've stopped," he exclaimed in disbelief.

"W-w-what happened," said Cassandra, half dead and bleeding from her arm stumps. The body of a dead snake lay beside her – its head crushed from a falling piece of luggage.

"Jack! He must have made it to the front of the train," said Stephanie who was picking herself off of

Sally. Her eyes glowed with the thought of her French Canadian gay man from the bar saving the day.

"Maybe your right," said Pinky, "but it sure took him long enough."

"Toby!" A yell from the back of the train made everyone turn. Vicky was standing over the limp body of her son. "Someone help! Oh god!"

"Let me through, let me through!" said Pinky, maneuvering over the fallen luggage towards Vicky and Toby.

"Oh, Pinky! Save him, use your CIA powers and save him, oh please!"

"He's okay!" Pinky said reassuringly to Vicky as he checked his pulse and breathing. "But he is unconscious from the fall. Let's give him some room, and he should come-to shortly."

"Oh! Toby, my son," a tear was streaking down Vicky's cheek. *Why wasn't I there for you!* Vicky's thoughts were heading back in time when she was only a girl. Back when she was ten her mother had fallen asleep and forgot to pick her up from school. Vicky had to walk the twenty mile trip down the dirt road back home all on her own. Grey, stormy clouds crowded the sky. Vicky decided, against better judgment, to walk through one of the old farmer's fields. *Just a little short cut*, she remembered thinking. But it was a deadly short cut. In the middle of the field, the old farmer had forgotten to fill an old well. The unknowing little girl walked straight overtop of the hole and fell right down to the bottom. *There I stayed, alone, cold and afraid for ten days*, Vicky remembered. On the eleventh day, the old farmer was walking by and heard her soft whimpering. She was near death – and it was all her mothers fault. Vicky would never let that memory go. She always kept Toby near by. *I have failed as a mother*, she was now thinking.

"There, there," said Pinky, who had his arm around Vicky, "he will be alright, I promise."

"You promise?" Vicky said, looking up into the deep blue eyes of her lover.

"Yes, my love, I promise. But their mushy moment was suddenly trampled by a more pressing matter.

"The snakes! The snakes are coming through!" Sally was pointing towards the door, which was knocked open during the sudden stop. Through it came the now familiar hissing of their venomous enemies.

"Quick everyone, to the back of the train!" shouted Pinky. "We've got to get off of this train!" Pinky's mind then turned to his mission. *Where is Taves?* He thought to himself. During the commotion he had forgotten to keep his eye on him. *I must remember my mission*, Pinky reminded himself. *I must remember to kill Harry Taves before he is allowed to escape.*

"Oh no!" came the horrified cry of the passengers aboard VIA rail 01. "We've come to a stop alright, but in the middle of a bridge!"

Sure enough, amidst the darkness spanned a magnificent bridge almost half a mile long and probably equally as high. Wondrously picturesque, the wooden trusses of the bridge also spelt disaster for the stranded passengers. The only path to freedom was marked by the thin timbers of the railway track. Between the timbers, the faint outline of a river at the bottom of a deep chasm could be made out. One false move and you would fall to your death.

19

WHO IS HARRY TAVES?

Harry Taves was not on board the train anymore. He was now running – running for his life. While everyone onboard the train was preoccupied with the snakes, Taves managed to sneak to the back of the train and open the rear exit hatch. Under the pale moonlight, Taves was awkwardly leaping across the gaps in the bridge, his chest heaving under the strain of his own weight.

How did I get into all of this mess, he was wondering to himself as he flew, *and how did they find me?* Taves was referring to the CIA agent Pinky Jordan. *I had been so careful, always covering my tracks. How did the CIA find out?*

It was clear the Harry Taves was living a mysterious double life. How had Taves managed to piss of both Janzo Kim, the Chinese multi-billionaire, and the government of the United States of America?

***

It started thirty years ago, when a young and slightly more attractive Harry Taves was finishing college. Like many young people, Taves couldn't find a way to use his college degree doing anything constructive – and so he joined the military. But his misdemeanor and inability to accept authority quickly landed him in latrine duties. He would spend thirteen hours a day simply scrubbing toilets. Taves had seen all manners of human excrement, and even fished his share of used condoms out of the toilets. Back in those days, gays weren't allowed in the military, but given there were no girls on base; Taves had to conclude that something dirty was going down – literally.

And that's how it went for Taves for the better part of three years. He was able to escape for some basic training every once in a while, but mostly his life was occupied with hours of scrubbing, rubbing, and covering up after homosexual affairs. He was miserable, and deep down, he was longing for more. He longed for a life of excitement, a life of intrigue, but mostly, a life fraught with danger. Harry Taves knew that he was meant to leave all of the "shit" behind him and move on to more dare devilish activities.

Then one day, while scraping away at a particularly unyielding piece of feces, Taves was interrupted by a shadow on the wall.

He turned to see a man standing in the door; a dark man; a rather mysterious looking man.

"Harry Taves,"

"Yes. Who are you?"

"What do you say we go for a walk?" the man half asked, half ordered.

Together the two of them made their way through Washington, past numerous famous landmarks, until eventually coming to rest at the Lincoln Memorial. They had a seat on the steps.

"You're an ambitious man, aren't you Mr. Taves?" the man inquired.

"I guess you could say that," Taves responded. "Right now my ambition is to find out who you are."

"I'm a man who has the power to turn your life upside down," the man replied. "That is, if you want your life turned upside down?"

Taves had never referred to it in that exact fashion, but he supposed the man was correct. He supposed the man might have something interesting to say. So Taves listened.

When their conversation was done, Taves knew that things were finally turning around. He knew that the danger he desperately craved would soon be in his grasp.

"So what do you say, Taves" asked the mysterious man. His arm folded across his chest in anxious anticipation.

"What the hell... let's do it!" said Taves, a smile forming on his lips for the first time in years.

"Then let me welcome you, my friend, to the CIA." The man offered his hand, which Taves gladly shook.

Taves' CIA career started out well. He met knew people, he shook important hands, and he even met a young woman – briefly.

But very soon, things were going to turn for the worst again.

One day, Taves' boss beckoned him into his office. There, he laid out the details for Taves' first mission overseas.

"Your mission, Mr. Taves, should you choose to accept it, is to infiltrate deep into enemy territory to spy on the infamous warload, Janzo Kim."

"Ah, yes I've heard of this man," said Taves, as he leaned over to look at a black and white photograph of the Chinese man in business attire.

"We need to know everything this man is up to. What he eats for breakfast, when he's taking a shit and who he's taking his shit with. All of it, Taves. This is a dangerous mission. Are you sure you are up to it?"

"I'm ready, boss," said Taves confidently.

"Good, then you will leave immediately. Good luck, agent Taves."

"Thank-you, sir!" Taves could almost scream with delight.

Two days later Taves was on a plane overseas.

Taves liked to fly. He liked the idea of being above the world, being above everyone else. It was how he had always looked at himself. Basic land travel, like on a train perhaps, made him feel low. It made him feel small in a world that he always felt wasn't big enough for him

Even on the trip over, even before his mission had officially begun, he was beginning to formulate in his mind for the next period of his life. Suddenly it was all falling into place.

Taves began small in Kim's organization. At first he had just been implanted in the mail room, doing simple filing and deliveries. He was able to gather some remote information through the mail, making copies of various letters and transferring them back overseas, but Taves knew, as did Langley, that the whole operation would be a timely process. Obviously many of Janzo Kim's more dubious dealings could not be accessed through the mail, and as Harry Taves gradually moved up the ranks within the Trinket business, the volume of the intelligence he was able to gather also increased.

Eventually, after two years on the job, Taves found himself on the "top floor" as it was called, working in very close proximity with the big man himself. Until then, Taves had only seen Kim speaking at various functions, and had even crossed paths with him out in the streets at various times, but the two had never met.

Their first meeting actually took place on the roof of the building, during a large masquerade ball. Officially the party was a fundraiser, but everyone knew it was also a chance for the ambitious up-and-comers to do some hardcore networking, and perhaps make an impression that might move themselves up the ranks. Taves and Kim's meeting actually ended up being rather cliché. Kim had a cigarette hanging from his mouth and was searching around in his pockets for a lighter.

Taves just happened to be walking by at this moment and quickly produced his lighter for the big boss.

"Allow me, sir," Taves offered. Kim calmly held his cigarette out and sucked in as Taves lit it up for him. Kim pulled back and took in one large and engrossing puff. He then pulled the cigarette from his mouth and sized up the man standing before him.

"I've seen you around. You're working pretty close to me these days," Kim said.

"That's right," said Taves, as coolly as he could muster. "The name is Taves, Harry Taves."

The two offered each other their hands. Little did both of them know, that simple hand shake would be the start of a series of events that can only be described as monumental.

Three years had passed and Harry Taves was still dutifully performing his mission overseas in China. He had worked his way into being one of Janzo Kim's closest confidants. He was gathering intelligence about Kim in mass quantities, including the fact that he was sleeping with his daughter, Saki Kim, but he was also beginning to wonder why he wasn't hearing from his government.

Unbeknownst to Taves, the CIA had actually sent Taves on a wild goose chase – a ruse designed to provoke the trinket market kingpin. Supposedly, the CIA didn't even expect Taves to survive more than one week. They had specifically recruited someone they thought would fail miserably and get themselves killed

Why aren't they responding to my transmissions? thought Taves at the time.

But after another year passed with no word from CIA headquarters, Taves realized that he had been used. *I was totally fucked over by those bureaucratic fuckshits!*

With the information he now had, and with his own government betraying him, it was time for Taves to put into motion the grandiose plans he had for his future. It was time to start working his agenda.

Taves was launched into a personal vendetta against the United States government. He used his every increasing skills in espionage as well as the federal secrets he gained over the years to launder millions of federal dollars into his personal bank account. He gained great power of his own accord, and when the timing was right, he turned the tables on Kim himself. He blackmailed the man with the knowledge of his daughterly affair and moved to Canada to start his own multi-million dollar business.

The experience left him jaded and scared. He lived a life of luxury; of money, high class prostitutes, and one damn good looking assistant named Sally. But on the inside, he was alone. Never again could he trust anyone but himself. His bitterness towards the world manifested itself deep inside him, turning him in a monster.

"From this moment on," he said, "the world will bow before me! HAHAHAHA"

***

Taves had made it to the end of the wooden train bridge. He looked back triumphantly, panting heavily from his physical excursion. *So long, suckers!* He cooed to himself.

Suddenly, the sound of an approaching vehicle interrupted the otherwise silent backdrop. Around the bend came a flash of light, then the steady hum of a jeep. And behind the steering wheel was a face Taves knew all too well.

We meet again, you bastard.

With nowhere to hide, Taves only had one choice – to turn around and go back *towards* the train he was running from. Not wasting anytime, Taves started to spring (more like frantic jump-humping) his way back to the train. Under the cover of the pre-dawn darkness, he managed to avoid the searching headlights of the approaching vehicle, and its driver Janzo Kim.

Taves quickly climbed up the ladder to the train's metal roof. His heart was racing, his lungs burning against the strain of the physical activity.

Once on the roof, Taves sought out a hiding spot between the observation car and the sleeper car. Now, safely out of sight, Taves wondered what was going to happen next.

If I run, I'll be captured by Janzo Kim

If I stay, I'll be captured by that CIA agent Pinky Jordan

20

THE GREAT FLOOD

Shamus was on the floor of the engine car. The force from the halting train had knocked him over as well. It had been a great struggle to stop the train, but pure adrenaline had given him the strength needed to pull the emergency break lever all the way down. With a train full of snakes, and the pending collision with an oncoming freight train, the train had to be stopped, and NOW! The passengers had no choice – they would just have to face the dangers of the Canadian wilderness.

Shamus got to his feet and brushed himself off. He scanned the car for any sign of something slithering. When he had gotten into the car through the window, he had been so occupied with saving everyone he hadn't even taken time to worry about himself.

Luckily there was nothing there besides the lifeless body of the engineer, Casey McTavish, lying before him. He concluded that all of the snakes must have made their way towards the back, herding the passengers from car to car. God he hoped there were survivors. If not, all of his heroics had been for nothing, and he had managed to get a helicopter pilot killed in the process.

Now what? Shamus thought to himself.

But he barely had time to think about it before his next course of action became abundantly clear. In an instant, and right before his eyes, the engine control panel burst into flames.

Shamus was knocked back for a second time, as he felt a wave of heat shoot over him. The entire room quickly filled with smoke, and the fire quickly began to spread, moving towards him.

Shamus retreated to the door, but then thought twice about moving into the adjacent car. There were snakes all over the place, and he couldn't take the chance. But he had to do something fast.

Instead, he opted to move back the window from which he had entered the train. He had to fight his way through a tuft of smoke before getting to the window and managing to stick his head outside, finally getting the chance to breathe some fresh air. But the fire was still moving towards him.

As quickly as he could, Shamus made his way out the window and leaped to the side of the bridge below. He landed with a thud, and narrowly avoided falling right off the edge and down to the river that lay hundreds of feet down.

Shamus exploded with coughs, trying to get all of the smoke out of his lungs. Even then, he was wondering what had just happened.

The quick breaking must have shorted out the engine.

"Shit!" Shamus bellowed when his coughing had ceased. He looked back at the window just in time to see the flames completely overcome the entire engine car. It didn't look like Casey's family will would get much of a choice – he was getting cremated.

Shamus hoped the train contained a sprinkler system. Otherwise, those people better get off the train, fast!

***

Pinky was the last one to enter the observation car - the last car on the train. He turned and shut the door behind him, once again blocking the snake's access to them. But for how long?

All the survivors gathered in the center of the car.

"Now what?" asked Vicky.

"Now we get the hell off this train," Pinky announced.

"But we're not in any town. We're still in the middle of the wilderness. How will we survive?" Cassandra interjected.

"It's a risk we're going to have to take," Pinky shouted back. "There's no stopping those snakes, and there is another train about to collide with us at any minute."

Everyone moved to the rear of the car and to the exit door at the very back of the train. Cassandra was especially weak at this point, so Stephanie and Sally were helping her walk. Unfortunately she didn't have the arms to place over their shoulders, thus the two female lovers were forced to hoist her by the waist.

Pinky was the first to the door. Outside the sun was finally beginning to rise. Morning was coming.

He wasted no time and immediately began yanking on the handle of the door.

It didn't budge.

Pinky hurriedly began to use all of his strength and pulled and pulled. But still the door refused to open.

"You've got to be kidding me," Sally said, utterly defeated.

"What the fuck is wrong with this thing?" Pinky shouted. "Open you mother fucker!" he bellowed at the door.

Pinky got desperate. He began pounding on the window in the door. He hit at it hard, but also weak. Pinky was nearing the end. He was losing it. He began to feel like the train had officially beaten him. They had all come so far, and now, with the trained stopped, and their escape finally pending, the door would not open. This wasn't happening.

Stephanie spoke up. "We have to find another way out. That train is coming."

Everyone else turned their attention to the windows, looking around for anything they could find that might shatter it.

But Pinky remained fixated on the door. He had his face pressed up against the window, hopelessly staring out the back of the train and down the tracks. About a hundred yards down through the dim light he thought he could make out the vague shape of another vehicle on the tracks.

The other train?

No, this vehicle was stopped. It wasn't moving. What, or who's, was it?

He quickly got his answer. Suddenly, and without warning, a face jumped into view in front of the window. It stared back at him. It stared with accusing eyes and bad teeth.

It was the face of a man. A man Pinky knew all too well. Pinky had never met the man, but he had seen many pictures of him. He had studied the man. He even liked to brag that he knew the man better than he knew himself.

He was the man who had technically hired Pinky for this mission, only it had all been done over the phone and by e-mail. They had never seen each other, and therefore, the man probably had no idea who he was looking back at. He definitely didn't know that Pinky was in fact a CIA agent, one who had infiltrated his operation for reason's that satisfied his own agenda.

The man was Janzo Kim.

Kim stared back at Pinky for what seemed like an eternity. Pinky didn't say anything. He was too thunderstruck. *What is he doing here?*

Finally, Janzo Kim spoke. "Have fun together, suckers!"

And with that, Kim turned and casually walked away. After an oceanic plane ride, many dealings, and the eventual highjacking of a rail car, Kim had shown up at Via rail 01 and literally "sealed" their fate. He had traveled so far for one simple and short lived act – to lock the door.

And that was it. He didn't care who else died. He only cared that Harry Taves died. Amazingly, Harry Taves wasn't even on the train.

Pinky had little time to process this irony before Vicky showed up at his back.

"Who was that?" she asked.

"That," replied Pinky, "was a very bad man."

"What?"

"And he is the one who locked the door. He has left us for the snakes," Pinky continued.

But now, the snakes weren't the only thing to worry about. Suddenly, Vicky felt a drop of water on her arm.

***

The scene inside baggage car was surreal. A dim light swayed gently back and forth under its own militia, cascading fleeting shadows of toppled luggage and slithering snakes. A faint orange light was peeling in from the one small window in the corner of the car; the morning light slowly revealing more and more of the hidden dark, slithering shadows.

Then, as if God himself grew tired of the eerie peacefulness, an eruption of water started to rain down from the ceiling. The train's automatic sprinkler system had been activated. The sound of falling water eclipsed all other sounds. A pool of water, now almost two inches deep, started to form on the floor. Slowly but surely, the baggage car started to fill up with water.

Only two minutes later the water was almost one meter deep. Beneath the murky train water, the mélange of reptilians began to swim. It was a beautiful sight: the dim glow of the rising sun piercing the dark shadows beneath the water. And the water kept falling. Soon it was almost at the ceiling. Had anyone been alive in this car, they would have surely died a horrible drowning/snake death.

The door connecting the baggage car to the coach car was now holding back several metric tons of water. Under the strain of weight, the door buckled and exploded outward. The water rushed through the opening, enveloping the once dry coach car. At the head of the tidal wave careening across the car were several wide eyed snakes – surfing closer and closer towards their tasty prey. It wasn't long until the coach car was also full of water. *Where was it all coming from!*

Again, only a small metal door was holding the water back from reaching the bar car, with its dome attachment. And again the metal door could not hold the weight of the expanding water pressure.

KA-POW!

The door exploded.

***

Everyone in the observation car heard a thud, and then a creaking.

"Now what?" said Vicky.

She got her answer.

In an instant, the sprinklers in the car engaged and began raining down onto the remaining six of them. Everyone was soaked immediately.

"There must be a fire," Cassandra shouted over the intense sound of the spilling water. "They come on automatically in every car."

"Great, but when do they stop?" Stephanie inquired. Cassandra didn't answer right away. She looked at Stephanie very seriously.

"They don't."

"What do you mean they don't?" said Stephanie.

Cassandra was now quick to answer. "They keep going until they are shut off manually from the engine car. There is supposed to be a drainage system opened in the floor, but it also has to be done from the engine."

The water was quickly beginning to pool on the floor. Vicky had Toby standing behind her. Her young son was reaching a boiling point of his fear. He had only recently regained consciousness, and was still a little out of it.

Everyone was.

But they had to keep themselves composed. After all they had been through, to give up now would was out of the question. Vicky wished Pinky held the same sentiment. He had taken a seat in a chair and just sat there staring, emptily allowing the water to rush over him. For the first time that evening, he was not the first one to throw out suggestions. He was very quiet, as if just waiting for the next catastrophe to come and overtake him. "Pinky, darling, what should we do," she asked quietly.

"What does it matter, we are all dead," Pinky said dejectedly.

"Damn it, Pinky, haven't we learned that perseverance can conquer any evil!?" shouted the Cassandra, her strong voice instilling confidence in the passengers.

"Ya, like the stump-lady said," said Toby, "we can do this. We can survive!"

"Well kid, I've got to hand it to you – you are a tough son of a bitch," said Pinky, "but how are we supposed to escape from this? We've got a train full of snakes trapped on a bridge with a freight train barreling out of control down the tracks towards us."

He didn't need to finish. They were all thinking the same thing – *and now we're facing drowing.*

Indeed, the future looked grim.

"Well, how about THAT!" said Toby, who suddenly saw what they must do. He was pointing towards a hatch on the roof of the train. Everyone had missed it, but not young Toby.

"Oh shit! It's an emergency exit!" shouted Cassandra. "I forgot, only the observation car has it."

"That was very…observant of you Toby," Vicky said to her son.

"We're saved!" seconded Stephanie.

The water was now pooled up to their knees.

"Ok, people. Let's grab some luggage and open that hatch!" instructed Cassandra. In unison, the remaining passengers worked to construct a wall of luggage that they could use to climb to the roof. Sally was the first one up. She pushed on the levers latching the emergency door closed. It opened easily. A blast of cool morning air pushed through the small opening.

"Quickly everyone! Let's go!" Sally said as she pushed herself through the hatchway and onto the roof of the train.

.

"What the F?" screamed Cassandra, who looked over just in time to see the door completely disintegrate, a wall of water revealing itself behind it.

"O-my-God!" yelled the passengers. *This was something out of a bad horror movie.*

In an instant, the water was rushing towards them. The five passengers still in the car were hit by the wave of water and knocked off their feet. The wall of luggage strained against the incoming weight of water. It wasn't long before it all came tumbling back down, leaving no way for them to reach the hatch fifteen feet above them.

Lurking beneath the water, the snakes started swimming towards the passengers. Stephanie was the first to see them.

"The snakes!"

Vicky hurriedly grabbed her son's arms and pulled him in close to her. It wasn't long before the water was waist deep, with snakes swimming all around them. The affects of the afrohottinessliaphane had clearly not worn off. There was still great sexual tension in the air, especially with the sight of two voluptuous females in wet shirts.

The snakes were immediately attracted to the tension and moved in on their prey. All the humans could do was bat them away. Toby splashed at a snake, which only made it angrier.

Pinky swam to a window and started kicking at it. He was hoping to burst the glass and make the water rush out, and hopefully the snakes. He was barely able to make a crack. They would just have to wait until the rising water brought them up to the ceiling.

"Everyone, we need to huddle together under the hatch," Pinky said, gesturing for the others to join him. The water was now too deep to stand in.

"Almost got him! A little higher!" Sally was yelling.

"I-I-I can't lift him any higher. Toby, you must jump!" Vicky was trying to instruct Toby to leap skywards, but he was still too out of it to respond in time.

A giant purple snake suddenly surfaced a few inches from Vicky. "Vicky! A snake is behind you! Watch out!" Cassandra shouted. But Vicky was busy trying to save her sons life.

Using her legs to kick her broken body through the water, Cassandra managed to propel herself between Vicky and the snake. The purple snake, wasted no time launching itself at Cassandra. Its sharp teeth pierced through her esophagus, sending her into a dizzying final spin before plunging beneath the water to her death.

Cassandra! You saved me! Vicky took one last deep breath, than launched herself upward through the rising water. The jump was just high enough. Toby was able to grab a hold of Sally's outstretched arms, who prompted lifted him to safety.

"You must go next, Vicky!" shouted Pinky. His hair was soaked as waves of water pulsed against his body. The water was now almost two meters deep.

"I can't, I don't have the strength," she responded softly. But the truth was much worse than that. A small snake had snuck up and bit her leg while she was saving her son. The venom wasted no time traveling through her blood stream. Vicky's vision started to blur and she slowly started to loose consciousness.

Realizing what was happening to the love of his life, Pinky finally snapped. "Fuck you snakes! Fuck you Harry Taves! And fuck you Janzo Kim!" Pinky took Vicky's failing body and swung it over his shoulders. He then swam upwards until his hand reached the emergency exit. With the power of two men combined, agent Pinky Jordan lifted himself through the hatch onto the roof. A warlike cry bellowed from his lungs as the strain of the working muscles tore right through his shirt.

Hot.

Without wasting anytime, Sally closed the hatch after Pinky and Vicky exited. They were now safe from the snakes.

Amidst the rising sunlight, Pinky laid Vicky's body down on the roof of the metal railway car. Her breathing was shallow and erratic. It did not look good.

"Vicky! You can't die, please! You mean so much to me!" Tears were flowing from Pinky's eyes as he grasped onto Vicky's hands with a defiant grip of belief.

"P-Pi-Pinky," stuttered the ailing woman, her breasts heaving up and down under her tight, wet shirt. "Take care of my son."

"Don't talk like that; you are going to make it!" stammered Pinky.

"Light...growing....dim......voice....starting...to fail....I....I....can see Jesus.....yes....he is ...calling me now.....good bye....my love....good bye my son.....good....b...b...b...." At 5:34 am, Vicky Patterson passed away on the roof of a train. Below her, a deadly pool of train water and snakes sloshed back and forth.

21

THE ASSASIN

The sun lifted its head above the horizon, blasting the surviving passengers with light as they sat atop the metal railway cars. Now only five survivors remained: Toby, Pinky, Sally, Stephanie and Taves. *But where had Taves disappeared to?*

A long silence full of grief and remorse was finally broken by Stephanie. "Pinky, what should we do now?"

The trauma of loosing a loved one clouded Pinky's head with thoughts of anger and regret. Finally, after a long pause full, Pinky responded. "This was my fault, this whole ordeal was my fault!" He managed to stammer, tears streaking down his cheeks.

"What are you talking about, this was not your fault! How could you have known?" Sally put her hand on Pinky's shoulder, and offered him a small smile of understanding. The truth was, however, she wasn't sure anymore who was to blame for this disaster. In fact, no one was sure what was happening anymore. Before the flood of snake filled water and the emergency stop, Pinky was about to tell everyone why a CIA agent was aboard the train. Then, all of a sudden, Harry Taves seemed to be running away. *Was Taves responsible for this whole ordeal?* Wondered Sally, memories of when she first met Taves came flooding back into her mind.

"No, you don't understand, this is all my fault!" Pinky managed to say.

"Why don't you explain what is going on here, Pinky, maybe that will help," said Stephanie, a tight knot of anxiety starting to build in her stomach.

"Yes, why don't you tell us what is going on 'Pinky'", came a mysterious, deep, Asian voice from behind them. The surviving passengers wielded around in time to see Janzo Kim ascend the metal ladder at the rear of the train, a black pistol positioned in his right hand.

"Who the fuck…." Sally started to say, but she was immediately cut off by Janzo Kim.

"Shut your mouth, you dirty whore," screamed Kim, his pistol now directed at Sally. "You will learn to speak when spoken to, bitch!" Kim's dark eyes penetrated deep into the eyes of the surviving passengers. One by one, he starred them down like a guard dog at a junk yard.

"What do you want, Kim," said Pinky, anger resonating deep inside his voice.

"What do I want?" said Kim, holding back evil laughter, "I want Harry Taves, that's what I want!"

"Pinky, you know this guy?" said Steph, and then "is this asshole the guy that locked us in the train?"

"Who are you calling asshole, ASSHOLE!" retarded Kim, his gun now trained against Stephanie's right temple. "And you! Who the shit are you?" Kim was motioning towards Pinky, a look of confusion crossing his face.

"I'm special agent Pinky Jordan, CIA," replied Pinky, his eyes matching the cold darkness of Kim's. Pinky had lost everything, he wasn't afraid of anyone anymore.

"CIA!" Janzo Kim let out an unattractive snort. "What are you doing here, you yank?"

"You know why I am here, Kim. I've come to put an end to your reign of terror on the free markets; to put an end to your *Chinese* trinket empire that has displaced the once strong U.S. markets; to stop you from running over this world with your bullshit and lack of remorse for the free world; I'm here to arrest you, once and for all!" Agent Pinky Jordan stood up from his fallen lover and leaned in close to Janzo Kim.

Kim could hardly restrain himself as he responded: "*Arrest* me! HA! And let me ask you how you plan to do that?"

"Like this! JUDO-CHOP!" and with a blindingly fast swipe of his hand, Pinky knocked the run clean out of Kim's hand. The gun fell with a loud clatter on the roof of the railway car, coming to rest a few meters away.

"Oh! I've had enough of this, prepare to die you American pheasant!

And with a loud war-like scream, Kim flew himself towards Pinky, their bodies colliding with tremendous force. Kim worked quickly to knock Pinky to the ground using one of his powerful Karate moves, but Pinky was ready with an equally quick counter punch to the nuts.

"ooooooooooooooooooahhhhhhhhhh!" yelled Kim, his eyes going cross-eyed from the pain. Pinky took the opportunity to land a perfectly placed round-house kick, aimed at Kim's head. But Kim was already planning his next move, and easily avoided the kick. With the force of many elephants, Kim again flew himself towards Pinky, this time catching him off-guard. Pinky fell down on the metal roof, the perforated stainless steel jabbing into his spine. Pinky let out a deep howl from the pain, while Kim rolled on top of him and started to punch. Blood spurted out of Pinky's mouth as a wave of punches peppered him.

"Stop! Oh please stop!" yelled the ladies from the sideline. But they weren't going to stop. Pinky

Jordan had waited his entire career to confront Janzo Kim, and he wasn't prepared to loose easily.

***

Pinky had first joined the CIA in 1984, a time when government secrets and suspicions proliferated throughout the administration. Back then, as Pinky often recalled, things were different. Spying on the enemy was a romantic lifestyle full of danger and sex. Deep inside underground military compounds, men with cigars ran the entire country without ever being seen by the public. If the average person was to learn about all of the threats to U.S. soil, public outbreaks of fear would engross the country. Back in 1974, few things mattered more than the economy and so keeping enemies poor and the public ignorant were top CIA priorities.

One wintery day in 1984, Pinky Jordan was handed his first assignment on Janzo Kim. The Chinese entrepreneur was radically altering the trinket market, selling gizmos and gadgets for many dollars cheaper than what could be produced in the U.S. and Canada. As a result, the U.S. economy started to fall into recession. The CIA wanted Kim taken out, and Pinky Jordan was the person selected to do the job. As it turned out, another CIA agent was quietly following Kim back in China – a man by the name of agent Harry Taves.

Not unlike the space agency, the CIA underwent severe budget cuts during the recession, and many thousands of secret CIA jobs and missions were put on hold – including Pinky's assassination mission in China. Months turned into years, and soon many people began to forget all about Janzo Kim and the lone agent following him, Harry Taves.

Then, one day in early spring, Pinky's boss announced that the mission would be reinstated. But, when the administration tried to get in contact with Harry Taves, they found that he was gone. Not only had he disappeared, but he had stolen large sums of government resources and plugged them in to his own business. Harry Taves had gone *rouge*! Soon after this revelation, the CIA realized that it had a major security threat on its hands: If Harry Taves leaked the information that Janzo Kim was once to be executed by the U.S. government, all hell would break loose and many thousands of men and women would loose their jobs as a result of a government inquiry. As well, Janzo Kim was continuing his massacre of the U.S. trinket market at a rate which would eventually lead towards economic collapse and the rise of China as the new super-power in the world.

In the summer of 1989, the CIA had a solution they thought would eliminate both threats with one stone: Kill Harry Taves and make it look like the Janzo Kim did it. That way, Kim could be arrested for "murder" and Taves would be out of the picture. Alas, many years passed by without action, as new staff inside the CIA administration raised red flags over the ethical implications for governmentally assisted assassination.

Then, by a thin stroke of luck, the CIA learned that Jazno Kim was already trying to kill Harry Taves, apparently for blackmailing him over pictures of Kim and his daughter doing-it. Kim, who learned of a business trip Taves was going on, placed a bomb aboard the plane Taves was supposed to be on. But, as we all know, that plan didn't pan out, as the Winnipeg police found the bomb before it got on the plane. Not wanting to waste this perfect opportunity to get back at Taves, Kim arranged to have the VIA train he was boarding filled with deadly snakes. Kim, who was in a panic, placed an ad on the internet for people who had access to the illegal drug *afrohotinessliaphane*. The CIA, not wanting to miss this opportunity, quickly responded to the ad, pretending to be an interested assassin; and Pinky Jordan was the man selected to fit the bill. Kim, thinking he was dealing with a professional assassin, promptly hired Pinky and relayed his plans. He also told Pinky where to get off the train so that Kim could personally meet him and exchange his payment of $1 million dollars Canadian. The plan was perfect, both from the perspective of Janzo Kim and Pinky Jordan.

You got all that? Good.

***

Back on top of the roof, the two men continued to swing punches at each other. Tired, bloody and gasping for air, the two men rolled on top of each other, grunting and hissing like wild animals.

"Stop, please stop!" Stephanie and Sally continued to beg in unison. Then a completely different voice was heard.

"Stop!" It was voice of Harry Taves, the black pistol in his hand. Taves had emerged from his hiding spot, and was now pointing Kim's fallen gun directly at Kim and Pinky.

22

THE NAKED TRUTH

"Harry Taves, so we meet again!" Janzo Kim said through gritted teeth.

"Shut up, you intestinal monster," retorted Harry Taves, the gun now pointed directly at Kim's head. "Or should I say, incest-ual monster!"

"You wouldn't dare...." Kim stepped forward, prepared to give his life to defend his dark little secret.

"Wouldn't dare say what," toyed Taves. "Say that you and your daughter, who is also your secretary, are doing it doggy style every Friday underneath your kitchen table?"

"You son of a bitch, I ought to...." but the angry Chinese man was cut off again.

"Go ahead, Kim, take your best shot. But little do you know that I'm actually an ex-CIA agent! So if you think that maybe I don't know how to operate a gun, then you are sadly mistaken." Harry Taves cocked his index finger slightly, to show that he meant serious business.

"That's it, asshole, you are dead meat!" and with that Janzo Kim lunged towards Taves, arms outstretched ready to kill his mortal enemy. *I have traveled half way across the globe for this moment, and I'm not about to fail because of some blubbering fatso and his little gun! I'd rather die!*

Taves pulled the trigger as Kim started to lung.

CLICK

CLCIK

"Uh oh...." Taves managed to say, before Kim landed on top of him, spilling the gun out of his hand. *The gun didn't fire! Shit!*

"Looks like your time has come, fatso!" Kim let out a lion-like roar and started throwing punches at Taves.

Looking on from a safe distance, Stephanie, Sally and Toby were shouting for Pinky to intervene. "Do something!" they cried, "you are a CIA agent for crying out loud!"

Pinky did not want to disappoint. After all, it was because of Janzo Kim that Vicky had died. All of his anger and guilt started to build and build until he was about to explode. He ran towards Taves and Kim and launched himself on top of Kim's back, sending him flying off of Harry Taves' body. Bruised and battered, Taves had the chance to get up after being pelted with punches. He went over to Pinky Jordan, who was now on top of Kim, and kicked his hard in the balls.

"OOOooooooooooooohaaaaaaaaaaaaaaaaaaaaaaa !" cried Pinky as he winced in agony. "My baaaaaaaaallllllllllllllllsssssss"

"That's for sending me to China for more than two years and never returning my phone calls!" Taves yelled, lining himself up for another ball-shot. But he never finished his kick. Janzo Kim had now gotten back up and, with blood streaming down his face, started to attack Taves again.

Pinky opened his eyes, tears drowning his vision because of the pain. In front of him, Janzo Kim and Harry Taves were battling dangerously close to the edge of the roof. More than 100m below them, the faint outline of a stream and some spruce trees could be made out. Pinky got to his feet and, fighting against the testicular pain, ran towards the two men once again. This time, he bowled right into them and sent them both careening towards the edge of the roof. Kim desperately reached for a handhold, but didn't find one. His momentum was now carrying him off of the roof towards a horrific falling-style death. Somehow, Kim managed to reach up at the last second and latch onto

Pinky's leg. The weight of Kim's falling body jolted Pinky down as well, and before he could realize what was happening, he too was starting to fall. Pinky desperately grappled for a place to hang on to, and found Harry Taves leg. Now Taves was falling, and just when it seemed he was about to fall off of the roof, a sturdy hand reached out and grabbed him by the wrist. Taves looked up, and was shocked to see a young man with blond hair looking down at him.

Shamus McGunty dug his heels in and pulled with all of his might. After stopping the train by pulling the emergency breaks, Shamus had made his away around the train to the rear, were he tried to enter the train. But he found that the train was actually full of water! Peering through one of the windows, Shamus watched in horror as he saw the body of a woman with no arms floating around in the water with snakes eating her eyeballs from their sockets! "You son of a snake!" Shamus had shouted. "You killed them all!" Shamus thought that maybe all of the passengers were already dead, but then he heard a commotion from the roof of the train and so he ascended the roof to investigate. There, he found two unbelievable attractive women, a young boy and three fighting men. Before he knew it, one of the men started to fall, who then grabbed onto the second man who then latched onto the third. Shamus jumped in just in time to grab that third man.

"Hold on!" Shouted Shamus to Taves, but Taves was busy trying to get rid off the two free loaders currently stretching his spine out by hanging onto his foot.

"Get off of my foot, you assholes!" he was shouting, in vain.

Below him, the CIA agent and Chinese business man were hanging on for dear life. Only one thought was on both of their minds: HANG ON OR DIE!

Above them, Harry Taves was trying desperately to shake them loose. He tried kicking, but that didn't work. *I have to loose them or else I will fall too!*

"I....Can't.....hold......much.....longer!" Shamus was starting to loose his grip on Taves' arm. *Hands...tooo...sweaty!*

In a move of desperation, Taves used his free hand to reach down and untie with shoe lace. Once untied, his shoe slowly started to slip off of his fat foot.

"No! No! wait don't do it!" Pinky was shouting, as he watched his only lifeline start to slip away. But it was too late, the shoe suddenly slipped right off of Taves' foot, and Pinky and Kim started to free-fall towards earth at a 9.8m/s/s. It took 20 seconds for the sound of their last scream's echo to diminish as it bounced back and forth across the canyon.

Relieved of two-thirds of the weight on his arms, Shamus was now able to pull Taves up and back onto the roof. Shamus collapsed back in a pile of sweat, exhausted from the physical exertion.

"Well thanks for saving me, buddy, but it was all for not! See that train over there?" Taves said, and sure enough in the not so far away distance the out-of-control freight train could be seen rapidly approaching. "We are all going to die now, its too late! We won't be able to make it off of this bridge in time. But at least I'll have the pleasure of knowing all of *you* will die along with me! HAHAHA."

BANG

Taves suddenly paused, a frightened look crossing his face. He took his hand and felt the back of his head and then look at his hand. *It was covered in blood!* "What the...." Taves turned around and saw Toby standing a meter away, a smoking gun in his hand.

"You forgot about the safety, mister," Toby said as he slowly lowered Kim's black gun down beside him.

"You....you....just....shot..... me?" Taves was starting to go dizzy; the pain from the bullet wound rapidly catching up with him.

"You bet I did. That's for stealing my Nintendo!" shouted Toby, and then added, "oh ya, and for killing mom and her boyfriend, too!"

"But....I....can't.......die?" Taves' knees buckled from under him and he fell right off of the railway car to his death in the gorge below.

"Oh my god, Toby!" shouted Sally. "You just killed him!"

"I know, sorry," said Toby. "But I really didn't like him!"

"Well that is no excuse for killing someone! I mean, sometimes I don't like people because I think they are annoying or smell bad, but that doesn't mean I just kill them!"

"You are right, I am ashamed of myself," said Toby, dejectedly. He started to raise the gun again, but this time he was pointing it at himself.

"No! Toby don't, you have too much to live for!" Sally shouted back. But Toby wasn't listening.

"Mommy, I'll see you soon," he said, and then fired a shot directly into his brain. Blood splattered all over the place. Steph and Sally both closed their eyes and screamed. Shamus couldn't believe what he was seeing. *What happened aboard this train!?* He was wondering to himself.

After a few seconds of silent mourning, Shamus broke the silence and said, "we have to go now, otherwise we too will be dead meat."

"But....but...but that train is only thirty seconds away, if that. We will never escape in time." Steph managed to say through the tears.

"I've got an idea, I need your shirts, quickly!" Shamus ordered.

"What?" Sally and Steph both said in unison, "why do you need our shirts?"

"I don't have time to explain! Listen, do you want to live or not? You have to trust me! Now, your shirts, quick!" *Time was running out.*

Sally undid her blouse and Stephanie unzipped her uniform tunic. Shamus grabbed them and started tying several knots.

"Now, I need your undershirts too! Quickly!" Shamus said, beckoning them to remove another layer of clothing.

Wow, this guy sure knows how to get things started! Thought Sally, as she took off her white undershirt. Her bare skin shivered against the cold morning air. Likwise, Stephanie also took off her shirt and handed it over to Shamus. She couldn't help but stare at Sally's beautiful body, her erect nipples pushing against her tight bra from the cold.

"Good, almost there, but I'm going to also need your pants!" Shamus was busy tying even more knots and folding the clothing into a larger and larger sheet of fabric.

Sally and Steph both answered the call and took off their pants.

"One more thing, I need your bras!" Shamus said, realizing he still needed a little bit more fabric.

"Oh come on now, this is just getting ridiculous!" Stephanie said.

"Look lady, ridiculous is getting plowed over by a train full of dynamite because you didn't listen to a guy who was trying to save you! Now, the bras!"

Men.

Sally took off her bra first, followed by Steph. The two women smiled at each other, each of them remembering their little came of scrabble-gone-wild. *That seemed like ages ago now,* they both thought.

"Damn, I still need some arm-loops!" Cursed Shamus to himself. "Ladies, I need those panties ASAP!"

The freight train was now only ten seconds away. The bridge was starting to vibrate due to the approaching weight of the massive diesel locomotives.

Sally and Steph took off their final layers; fully exposed on top of a train on top of a bridge in the middle of the wilderness. How cool is that.

"Okay, I think it is ready!" said Shamus.

"What did you make," asked Sally.

"It is a parachute!" Answered Shamus, triumphantly.

"What?" said Sally in horror. "That will never hold us up?"

"Well it darn well has too, lady. We've got to jump, now! Okay, you come over here and your over here," Shamus ordered the two naked blonds to hang onto him from each side. He then took his belt and made a quick harness, which then went around their three waists. He then wrapped his hands around the panty-style-arm-holds. "Ready?" He shouted.

"You must be crazy!" said Steph.

"We are going to die!" cried Sally.

"Here we go!" shouted Shamus, as he jumped forwards off of the train into empty space.

23

DOWN, DOWN, DOWN

The next ten seconds happened in extreme slow motion. The speeding freight train full of dynamite and petroleum plowed head-on with the parked VIA rail passenger train on top of the bridge. A shockwave rippled through the metal railway cars, as rivets were popped out at the speed of sound. The iron couplings and trucks that kept these giant cars on their tracks for so many years disintegrated instantaneously into iron powder. Any glass was instantly shattered into a billion little pieces and sent scattering in all direction. The two locomotives rammed together with such great force that the giant fuel tanks aboard them instantly ruptured. The heat from the compression generated a spark which instantly spread to the leaking diesel fuel. A massive explosion ensued, generating a giant mushroom cloud of debris and smoke. Then, as the explosive shockwave traveled back through the freight cars, more and more explosions followed. The boxcars, stacked high with dynamite, exploded with such great force that the entire boxcar actually flew upwards and off of the bridge. The black steel tanker cars, full of petroleum products, blew their tops off and sent giant shards of steel in all direction. The forward momentum continued well after the first few explosions, and railways cars all over the place were forced to go up and off of the bridge. The bridge itself was straining from the weight of the two trains and the shockwave of the blast. Some of the supporting struts started to give, and then, just a few seconds later, the entire bridge came thundering down piece by piece. Many of the railways cars from the freight train were not even on the bridge, but the weight of the falling boxcars and tanker cars to which they were attached pulled them along for the ride. Down, down, down came the seemingly indestructible bridge.

As the first pieces of train and bridge hit the bottom of the canyon, secondary explosions were triggered. The explosions were of such great heat and force that they fused any distinguishable piece of metal together into one giant carcass of dead train. One by one, tanker cars and boxcars full of hazardous and flammable products were dragged down to their grave, 100 meters below. 100 freight cars, 100 explosions.

BANG!

KABOOM

CRASH!

KABLOOMY!

CRSSSSSSSSSHHHHHHHHHHH!

Naturally, this continued on for quite some time. After each explosion, a deafening blast followed and echoed against the canyon walls. A wall of fire and smoke soon reached almost as high as the canyon itself.

The last car on the freight train, the lonely old caboose, was also the last car to fall down the canyon. The shiny red box once held the train's switchman, but now it was used only for show. As the caboose fell, its shiny red paint glistened against the morning sun. It seemed to almost float there indefinitely. Down, down, down. And then *nothing*.

24

WHAT A VIEW

Just before the trains collided and exploded into *nothingness*, Shamus, Sally and Stephanie had jumped – all of their trust in a McGivor type parachute made by Shamus in about ten seconds.

At first, the three falling bodies fell like a rock. The tattered clothing strained against the rushing air. But soon, Shamus had managed to flatten out the clothing chute so that it was holding more air. Their decent started to slow, and soon they were gliding quite comfortably in the cold morning air.

"Oh my...." Shouted Steph and Sally, their boobs bouncing up and down as they descended.

"Oh my..." echoed Shamus, watching their boobs bounce up and down as they descended.

And then the explosion happened.

The first part of the explosion to reach the threesome was a hot blast of air and a defining sound. Then the threesome was propelled forwards with great speed as a wave of hot air and shrapnel caught up with them. As they tumbled forward, the parachute got all tangled up! Struggling to keep them on course, Shamus frantically pulled the panty-levers up and down. With the parachute tangled up in knots, the threesome started to free-fall again. *If Shamus didn't fix the chute in time...*

A massive explosion rocked through the canyon as the bridge started to fall apart. A giant cloud of dust and smoke covered everything. And for a brief period of time, the three-falling naked people disappeared from view.

And then, despite all odds and physics, the faint outline of two naked female bodies, a man and a parachute made of shirts and pants came into view. They had done it! They had regained control!

The threesome continued to glide towards the earth. All around them, the golden glow of the morning sunlight against the stands of spruce and pine shone the way towards a safe landing. "Look, over there!" Shouted Shamus, against the howling wind. He was pointing towards a small beach up ahead. Shamus yanked one of the panty-levers to the right and the other to the left. Slowly, the make-shift parachute turned to the heading of the small beach.

"Oh, it is so beautiful!" Said Sally, looking around at the wild Canadian landscape.

"It is so much larger than I thought!" said Stephanie, admiring the vastness of glowing foliage around them.

A few meters above the ground, Shamus pulled hard on the panty-levers to retard their decent. "Bent you knees!" he shouted. The three of them landed softy on the fine sand, the parachute collapsing beside them in a tangled mess.

"Wow!" Exclaimed Sally, "that was amazing! Thank you so much, Mr...." she realized that she didn't even know who this guy was. He had appeared out of nowhere and selflessly put himself in harms way to save them.

"You can call me Shamus," he replied, a warm smile crossing over his face.

"Thank you, Shamus," the women said, embracing his stone-carved figure.

"Hey Sally! I just remembered something!" said Steph.

"What's that?"

"You remember what Pinky was saying, about that special chemical that induces hornyness?"

"Yes, I remember," said Sally, a look of confusion crossing over her face. *Why did this matter now?*

"Well, you remember when he said that after half an hour, its affects wear off?" Steph continued.

"Oh, yes I do remember that!" said Sally, starting to realize what this meant.

"Well, I'm still extremely horny for you!" said Steph, "which means that my love for you is genuine! We were not under the influence of the drug when we did it!"

"Oh! You are right! I am also still horny! It must be true love!" Sally exclaimed, reaching out to embrace her lover.

Wow, thought Shamus, who had grown up on a small farm outside Winnipeg, *I've never seen anything so beautiful in all my life*. A tear flowed down his cheek.

And then the three of them totally did it on that beach, and it was totally awesome.

25

TEN YEARS LATER / EPILOUGE

"Honey, can you throw me the car keys?" Shamus McGunty called out.

"What's that, dear?" replied Sally from the bathroom.

"Don't worry, sweetheart, I've got it," said Stephanie from the kitchen. "Are you going to pick up Junior from hover-ball practice later, or should I?"

"Nope, I can do it!" Said Shamus, halfway out the door. "I want to show our little gaffer how to throw a curve-ball!"

"Oh, Shamus, our son is only eight years old!" sighed Sally, emerging from the bathroom with a towel around her head. "How do I look," she then asked.

"You look wonderful, dear," said Stephanie.

"Truly stunning sweet heart," added Shamus. "Okay, good-bye the loves of my life," he said as he exited their house and drove away in his Mercedes hover-mobile.

"Good bye husband," Steph and Sally said in unison.

"You know what I'm looking forward too?" asked Stephanie, her lips pursing together the way they do when her thoughts turn dirty.

"What's that, sweetums?" said Sally, who emerged again from the bathroom, but his time with no towel.

"I'm looking forward to making another one!" Steph said, referring to their plans to make another baby soon.

"Well, we should book an appointment then," said Sally. *Modern science has evolved so much in the last ten years*, she though to herself. Now, babies could be conceived in the laboratory with two eggs and one sperm. This coincided with the sharp rise in polygamy after world war three and the fall of the United States of America as a super-power because the world supply of oil ran out.

"What should we name her?" asked Stephanie.

"How about Sandra?" said Sally.

"No, too old-fashioned."

"How about Sophie?"

"Hmmm," considered Stephanie to herself, "yes, I like that! Sophie! Sophie McGunty-Warlock. I think that has a nice ring to it."

RING, RING, RING!

Their thoughts were interrupted by the video-phone.

"Computer: activate video-phone and display this wall," Sally called out, touching her finger against the wall nearest her.

"Connecting......transfer complete." Said the computer.

"Oh, why hello Mr. Prime Minister!" said Sally, as the video-screen flashed up on the electro-wall.

"Hello Sally! And hello Stephanie!" The Prime Minister said. "And how are we doing today?"

"Just fine, thank you," said Stephanie. "And what brings you by this lovely afternoon?"

"Well, ladies, I'm afraid it isn't good news at all. You see, we've had another incident. I'm afraid we are asking for your help once again." The Prime Minister's face went sullen. He then added, "I'm sorry I have to ask you this, but you are our best agents and we can't do this without you."

"Oh Mr. Prime Minister, we are married now and have a son. We can't just pick up and leave again! And remember what happened last time..." Sally was interrupted by the man.

"Please Sally and Stephanie, the nation is depending on you! Canada's freedom is at stake. I'm going to send you the full details via a secure teleconnection channel, stand by!" The Prime Minister disappeared from view.

Suddenly, a blue glow appeared in front of the two women. A second later, a binder labeled "top secret" appeared.

"Got to love this new instant hyper-mail," said Sally.

"Read this, and then let me know as soon as possible when you can depart! Over and out!" The screen flickered and then faded back to the color of the rest of the wall.

"Oh dear," sighed Sally. "What ever shall we do?"

"It says here that an American terrorist is alive, and the Canadian intelligence agency (CIA) reports that he is going to try and put snakes on a cruise ship!" Said Stephanie, after reading the first few pages of the report.

"Remember what happened last time the American terrorists tried that, don't you?" warned Sally.

"How could I forget, those snakes almost killed us had it not been for Shamus." Stephanie remembered when she had worked undercover aboard the old VIA rail train that ran from what-was-once-called Winnipeg to the-then-much-smaller-version of modern day Toronto.

"But at least we'd get a nice vacation …" considered Sally.

"And we'd get to wear our bikinis," added Stephanie.

THE

END

?

Printed in Great Britain
by Amazon.co.uk, Ltd.,
Marston Gate.